The Rise and Fall of the Egalitarian Fantasy

The Rise and Fall of the Egalitarian Fantasy

Genes, Biology and The Crisis Of Western Modernity

Brian Pottinger

ISBN: 1511508930
ISBN 13: 9781511508933

The Rise And Fall Of The Egalitarian Fantasy
An Essay On Genes, Biology and the Crisis of Western Modernity

*The ultimate effect of shielding men from the
effects of folly is to fill the world with fools ---
Herbert Spencer (1820 - 1903)*

Author's Note

THIS ESSAY EXPLORES one of the most important yet ignored links in modern history: that between the developed world's current social, political and economic structures, on the one hand, and what science is now telling us with compelling urgency about the innate nature of human beings, on the other.

There is an exponentially increasing volume of research and writing on the science of genetic and biological influence in the formation of human character and the nature of groups, whether defined by class, gender, race or nationality.

Similarly, there are countless recently-written books about the travails of the developed world; post facto explanations of why we find ourselves in a position of protracted financial turbulence, military impotence and social confusion.

Yet few have made the obvious connection, to ask the inevitable and deeply uncomfortable questions:

- What does our vastly expanded scientific understanding of our innate being tell us about the world we have created about us?
- Are our social formations in tune with that understanding? Is the unshakeable western belief in egalitarianism viable?
- Do we need to rethink our most fundamental assumptions?
- Have our ideologically and emotionally driven commitments to the noble concept of "equality" blinded us to the limitations imposed by genes and biology?

- And, most important, has this ideological blindness created not a fairer and kinder world but a more sinister and frightening one?

For those who already suspect this Essay is some philosophical or party political exegesis, worry not. It attempts in the most explicit terms possible to link genetic and biological research to the social, political and economic world about us. It argues that the still noble aspiration of egalitarianism has morphed into an Egalitarian Fantasy at odds with what the science today is telling us about ourselves. The disjuncture, always present, has now reached a critical point. For the sake of the next generation, our children, we no longer have the luxury of evading the tough questions.

This Essay argues that we cannot afford to ignore the reality of innate differences between individuals and groups in capabilities, capacities, attitudes, aptitudes, character and behaviour. Our failure to accept that reality has exacerbated inequality, weakened Western competitiveness, caused great injustice to the weakest amongst us and created an arc of chaos from the western most parts of Africa to the eastern most parts of Europe. It has also precipitated the most bitterly divisive political contestation within nations in recent Western history. We must deal with those realities: and now.

This is not so as to elevate one group above another, nor to set one society against another, never to claim moral ascendancy for one party over another, but the reverse, honestly to address difference, to respect it, to mediate it and to create stronger and more competitive, harmonious and fair Western nations at the end of it. It is precisely because of the failure of the Western elites for many decades to engage this debate, to even admit the salience of difference, that we are now confronted with such social discord, confusion and popular anger.

Why call *The Rise and Fall of The Egalitarian Fantasy* an Essay? Because that is what it is. It does not set out to be a scientific treatise. It is a polemic, but one girded with supporting evidence. In this I have drawn extensively on the work of people far more knowledgeable than I in the sciences of genetics, biology, genetic and biological evolution, neuro-genetics, neurology and all the other aspects of this vast, exciting and recently opened world. I do not for a moment expect them to identify with the wider social and political conclusions I have drawn from their work; that is my responsibility alone. I thank them, nevertheless, for the noble enterprise in which they are engaged. For only from truth can lasting understanding come.

I feel I can write with some knowledge on the topic of difference. As a South African journalist, I reported over many years that country's epic march to non-racial democracy. I have been struck by a simple anomaly ever since. Apartheid sought to entrench difference by Law. The Egalitarian Fantasy sought to abolish it by Law. Both failed at an enormous human cost.

Lastly, why have I, a person fortunate enough to have achieved virtually all my life's ambitions long before my expectations, chosen to enter this most explosively freighted debate? Because somebody has to: and now.

As always, my thanks to my wife, Susan, whose support, comments and interest have been a mainstay. Special thanks to my cousin, Ken Pottinger, whose delightful home in the south of France was the site of much debate, industry and agonising as we worked to turn a complex idea into a publication.

Brian Pottinger
Cornwall
March 2015

SOME DEFINITIONS

What is An Egalitarian Fantasy?

It is a belief that:

- We are all born the same and equal in our capabilities in all things at all times.
- We see everything the same way.
- We will react to circumstances in exactly the same and predictable pattern.
- We can all seize opportunity when presented in the same way.

The Rise and Fall of The Egalitarian Fantasy, argues that this way of thinking is against science, history and common sense. That it has caused huge problems in Western societies and pain to many people, groups and nations least able to defend their interests.

The Essay is NOT:

- An argument that people or groups should be castigated because they are different.
- A justification for unfair discrimination against anybody.
- A denial of the right of people to equality before the law

- A suggestion that one individual or group is morally superior to another
- A call for the negative stereotyping of individuals and groups.

It IS:

A call to political leaders to acknowledge and respect the importance of innate differences between individuals and groups so as to build fairer and more socially cohesive societies and a more understanding world.

An obvious question arises. Merely by talking about innate difference are we not laying a platform for unscrupulous people to justify the repression of others? Do we pave the way for another Hitler?

The answer is no.

First: It is a scientific reality that we cannot escape.
Second: Because we have ignored it for so long, we have led ourselves into troubled waters everywhere.
Third: Evil people have misused scientific discoveries throughout history. It is up to good men and women to ensure they do not misuse this one.

And that is the point of The Rise and Fall Of The Egalitarian Fantasy.

INTRODUCTION

In the years immediately after World War II, the political and intellectual leaders of the developed world sought explanations for the unique evil of the Nazi state. They fingered two culprits: nationalism and the appalling ideological use the Nazis had made of genetic differences between humans.

To counter the former they chose to create a federal Europe, drawing the member countries so closely together that none dared attack the other. That ideal is now challenged by economic reality and the irreducible forces of national, economic, cultural and biological difference. In dealing with genes, the developed world leaders took an even more fateful decision: genes and genetic differences between individuals and groups should play no role at all in post war life.

So they discouraged research, discussion or consideration of the role of genetics or biology in the life of individuals or, more broadly, in classes, groups, races and nations. They frowned on stereotypes or even humour based on genetic difference. They passed laws to jail people who referred to genetic difference in a way that they considered hurtful or hateful. Eventually and inevitably, it became a taboo subject.

The unshakeable core belief of the post-war era was that we are all born equal and can seize equally the opportunity to be successful. Equality of outcomes was thus a certainty if only equality of opportunity could be assured. The fact that some people were rich and successful and others were poor and unsuccessful, generation after generation, was not primarily due to inherited genetic or biological capacity, or lack of it, but to a skewered social order.

From this emerged the contemporary post modern Western European state: at its core it was socialist, redistributive and welfarist. The disagreements within the developed world's politics, whether billed as Conservative, Liberal, Labour, Socialist, Democrat, Republican, Social Democratic, Christian Democrat or anything else, were ones of degree, not principle. The egalitarian principle was inviolable.

There was one problem. Neither empirical evidence nor science could justify it. The founding assumption was flawed. It was based not on fact but on fantasy, an Egalitarian Fantasy.

This Essay proposes that the centrality of genetic and biological influence in humans and groups has been forcefully reaffirmed by the recent leaps forward in the neurosciences, biogenetics and in evolutionary genetics and biology. We now have a far better understanding of human nature and the way it drives our social, political and economic formations. We better understand that the age-old divide between nature and nurture is infinitely more nuanced than we have hitherto been allowed to believe.

Only now, with a wealth of new scientific evidence rolling out on an almost weekly basis, can we begin fully to grasp the conceptual cul de sac into which the developed world's political and academic elites have led us in the last six decades through their refusal to concede the importance of genetic and biological heritability in our existence. This denial has led directly to the eclipse of Western economic competitiveness while creating a climate of confusion, insecurity and loss of internal cohesion throughout the developed world.

Into this void, inevitably, have stepped the emergent forces of history represented by China, Russia, India and front-running developing nations. Unencumbered by this Egalitarian Fantasy, they are writing new realities based on an understanding of human nature as it is rather than the way we think it ought to be. It is these realities which at best risk side lining, or at worst, overwhelming, the developed world.

This Essay is a plea for developed world societies and their leadership to accept the importance of genetic heritability and to use the extraordinary gift that science now places in our hands to marshal our most priceless asset, human excellence, while still enabling every individual to advance as rapidly as possible to their fullest *genetic* capability. It is an appeal for us to strive towards creating strong, competitive and fair societies which work with these newly rediscovered, indeed timeless, realities rather than ignoring them or, worse, denying and repressing them.

Only two guarantees for equality can be credibly given. One is the equality of all before the law and the second is the equality of the moral being, however one chooses to conceptualise the latter. The former is within the power of humans to ensure; the latter is within the power only of the individual to achieve. Yet the course of western history since World War II has been to extend all sorts of declaratory rights and guarantees, nearly all of them now found wanting because of the implausibility of The Egalitarian Fantasy.

Elites have through time sought to impose their sets of values and objectives on everybody else, both within their own countries and abroad. In recent decades, however, Western elites have fatally confused the concept of equality with the idea of sameness. For them, equality can only be achieved through sameness. Where the project has run into difficulty --- and it has everywhere --- the response has been to trade down to the lowest common denominator. Equality, sameness and mediocrity have become synonymous.

The consequence of all this is injustice on an epic scale as those without the genetic capability to meet the expectations demanded by the Egalitarian Fantasy are consigned into welfare dependence and hopelessness. Those who exceed the expectations, conversely, are pulled down like crabs in a bucket; reduced to an emulsified uniformity and mediocrity. Only the very rich or the very bright escape.

The same arrogance abroad, the refusal to understand and respect the nature of human difference, has led to bloodshed and degradation in countries caught in the remorseless battle between tradition and modernity; what the French poet Guillaume Apollinaire called in the early 20th Century, in different circumstances, the quarrel between "order and adventure". A new form of Western moral imperialism, in some ways more destructive of communities than 19th Century colonialism, has destabilised nations from the western most regions of Africa to the eastern most parts of Ukraine.

In all of this, a new victim is emerging, neither imagined nor fabricated, the ordinary hard-working person trying to make a way in life and do the best for his or her children in a world that for many people has lost its connection with either reality or common sense. It is to these real victims that this Essay is dedicated. Its message is simple: only by understanding and respecting the reality of our genetic differences and the innate inequality of our natures, as individuals and groups, can we hope to create a world which offers the best hope for individual fulfilment and for general social betterment.

I begin this Essay by exploring the contribution science is making to our understanding of human nature; the variance between that understanding and the contemporary political and social consensus in the developed world; the five steps which have led to the incipient irrelevance of the developed world because of the Egalitarian Fantasy; the growth of *supercrisis.org* and its massively distorting effect on rational economic and social policy; the economic consequences of the Egalitarian Fantasy; the productivity conundrum and the impact all this has had on increasing rather than mitigating, inequality.

Thereafter I will look at the impact on society of specific consequences of the Egalitarian Fantasy such as extremist feminism, mass migration, frozen economies and the impact on family, cultural and social values. The political consequences of all aspects of the Egalitarian Fantasy are dealt with in the section that follows thereafter, including the break down in the element of reciprocity and thus trust in developed world societies, features that have led directly to our current and pervasive institutional crises.

The West's stewardship of a two-decade-long unipolar world while seized by the Egalitarian Fantasy is considered next and measured by the arc of disastrous Western interventions in the internal affairs of other countries from Afghanistan to Ukraine, all of them predicated on the fatal egalitarian conceit that all societies are the same and should and must be just like ours. Of course other politico-economic-geo-strategic issues are also factors here but beyond the scope of this essay.

Matters have come to a head economically with the Great Financial Collapse of 2007/8 and geo-strategically with the establishment of the self-styled Islamic State and the return of the Cold War, the ongoing aftermaths of which continue to provoke deep social and political insecurity. As this Essay will observe, there are recent signs throughout the developed world of a push back by ordinary people, bolstered by science and common sense, against the Egalitarian Fantasists and the social, economic, moral and political morass they have created.

The last part of this essay will urge a return to the core and traditional values which once underpinned the strength of the developed world.

SCIENCE VS THE EGALITARIAN FANTASY

Revolutionary advances in the neurosciences and its multiplicity of offshoots, in behavioural genetics and in evolutionary biology and psychology, now show persuasively that we are not all innately equal and similar; indeed we are different and often unequal in our capacity, capability, intelligence, competence, personality traits, temperament and character. People may be good in one thing, but not another. This is such a truism that it is remarkable that it has to be stated, but such is the nature of the debate.

These differences are very largely down to inherited genes which researchers now believe account on average for 40% of the differences in the various innate abilities and traits between individuals. The influence of so-called shared experience, in other words family, contributes a mere 10% to determining differences in ability; unique experiences such as illness, school or peer group account for about a quarter and the remaining 25% is held to be "measurement error" in which, of course, may still lie considerably more genetic influence than we can currently ascribe. The extent to which genes contribute to the difference in *specific* traits or competences in individuals, varies significantly. Research suggests that in some cases such as a predisposition to mathematical or scientific ability, it may account for as much as 70% of the difference.[1]

Thus genetic and biological influence, far from being negligible as we have been led to believe through years of misinformation, is crucial and perhaps determining in life's outcomes for individuals and, I will later argue, groups and nations. The influences capable of external or social manipulation are still important but the room for human intervention is limited to an extent not previously appreciated or admitted. The heart of the post-modern developed world consensus is accordingly challenged, as are the millions of individuals who up to now have misguidedly benefited from that ill-founded consensus.

All of these propositions are of course politically and emotionally freighted. Used cavalierly, they may strike at a human's sense of self-worth and optimism. They may open arguments by malicious groups that individuals and whole groups should be typecast, slotted into a hole from which they should never emerge. Again, they might lead to the suggestion that because people have the innate predisposition to behave a certain way, they should take no responsibility for behaving differently or for attempting to achieve anything in their lives.

So at this stage I need to make all the necessary qualifications to avoid the pointless diversions that are sadly so endemic in any contemporary discussion about the highly-charged subject of what Shakespeare originally and presciently identified as **nurture versus nature.**

- First, this Essay will not claim that genes alone influence the characteristics of individuals and groups. It will suggest that genes and biology have a huge role in establishing the *difference* between individuals and groups. Our refusal to accept that has led us into dangerous waters.

- Second, there is no such thing as a single gene which determines a particular outcome, whether it be virtuosity in music or criminal propensity or a temperament for just getting along. There are, however, packages of genes which invest individuals with various aptitudes or lack of them which in turn predispose individuals towards success in their lives or the absence of it.

- Third, this Essay will not claim that genetic influence is uniformly dominant in all phases of the life of the human individual. The research suggests genetic influence in accounting for the differences in personalities rises from 20% in infants to as much as 80% in people past middle age.[2] The inference is clear: if genetic influence has any chance of being mitigated by social intervention, it will have to be done early on in the life of an individual and, conversely, there is little point in seeking to ride

rough-shod over genetically embedded characteristics amongst adults as individuals or groups or
nations.

- Fourth, crucially, there can be no suggestion that
any individual born into a gender, class, race, nation
or group will automatically present all or even any of
the aspects which on average characterize that group.
Individuals may be *predisposed* towards a certain outcome because of membership of a group but it does
not mean they are *predestined*. We know through historic record, for example, that until recently at least
10% of people born into the bottom socio-economic
quintile in the developed world rose every generation into a higher socio-economic group.

- Fifth, this Essay will not suggest that humans as
individuals or as groups are frozen in the aspic of
their personal or national genotype (their genetic
template) or phenotype (what they become after
all the other influences including environment are
added). That is counter-intuitive and also against
the historical and biological record. We now know
that the human genome, the complete set of DNA
plus all its genes, is in a state of constant evolution.
At least 14% of that evolution has occurred in the
last 5 000 to 30 000 years.[3]

But to ignore existent personal and group genotypes
is equally fallacious. One cannot impose one-size-fits-all

solutions without regard to those differences as they currently exist and have so existed for millennia. Where it has been done, as this Essay will record, the consequences for individuals, groups and the West has been damaging.

Finally, perhaps most important of all, the mere recognition of differences born of genetic and biological influence does not imply a moral judgement about those differences. Two World Wars should be ample proof that the artistic or technological success of a nation is no guarantor of either the reasonableness or morality of that nation. If anything, the recognition of innate success attributes in individuals and groups places a greater, not lesser, burden on them to behave conscientiously.

The reality of genetically and biologically embedded differences between individuals has long been accepted. Less settled is the question of whether genes dictate differences in groups, particularly in racial or ethnic terms. This subject remains intensely emotional, so much so that many otherwise quite rational people bluntly refuse to even entertain the notion of something that could be considered an innate group characteristic or "group genotype": they prefer to call it a stereotype and abjure it. Embarrassingly, our new grasp of human nature is revealing that what once were called stereotypes often offer a better predicator of personal and group characteristics than all the politically correct psycho-socio-babble of recent decades.

The subject of genes and humans is so sensitive that some people in the scientific world believe we should stop research into the relationship between genes and race or gender entirely. Others suggest it should be allowed but not communicated. Fortunately for common sense and the integrity of science, a poll by *Nature* magazine in late 2014 showed the censors were outnumbered eight to one by those who believe the research should go ahead within established ethical frameworks and that it should be publicised.

Yet such is the power of this censorious minority with their mischievous, invidious and baseless comparisons between modern genetic research and the long discarded and discredited Nazi-style eugenics, that a suffocating pall has for decades been thrown over the subject. Some research projects in sports genetics, for example, avoid the use of the term genetics at all, preferring to refer to molecular biology and protein synthesis to forestall the negativity that research in genetics still attracts.[4] Other researchers avoid the inclusion of certain racial groups or severely under-represent them so as to sidestep what could be considered controversial research outcomes. Thus does the long tail of disinformation laid decades ago by the Fantasists, still stalk modern science.

One can understand part of the concern of the scientists. Too often have very nuanced and still tentative hypotheses been shorthanded by the popular media into headline controversy. But this reticence is still an ultimate cowardice and of no help to either science or the communities involved.

Even scientists quite prepared to accept the importance of genes and biology in the creation of individual characteristics, quail at the thought of making the leap to proposing genetic differences between groups. The latest cop-out has been to suggest that it is not the groups that display identifiable characteristics but only individuals within the group who present traits which are generally and observably similar.

Thus there may be differences in individual genotypes and although these differences may suggest a collective characteristic, it cannot be considered a group genotype. People may be allowed to differ *within* a group, but collectively they cannot be allowed to differ *as* a group. Even respected historians rely on the nonsense argument that because there are differences in IQ levels between groups within nations, it follows that IQ comparisons between nations are meaningless.

The foremost proponent of the view that there was no such thing as human groups, specifically racial, was the evolutionary biologist Richard Lewontin who in 1972 produced research which indicated there were more differences within populations than between them. This view diverted debate on the issue for nearly thirty years. Sadly for Lewontin and his adherents, the explosion in both the quantum and quality of genomic information since, has weakened his case. There is indeed as much that establishes differences between groups as does between individuals within them.

Others archly suggest that what exists is not differences between, say, races but differences in ancestry, an intelligent get-out-of-jail card for attempting to deal with one of the most ideologically laden issues of our age. People who regard themselves at the top of the pile are a great deal more accommodating of the notion of difference than are people who feel themselves at the bottom. This is perfectly understandable but it is not science and it is certainly not the basis on which to craft public policy.

At first, the very notion of differences in IQ between groups was disputed on the grounds that there could be no such thing as a culturally neutral way of testing and comparing intelligence. When that obstacle was dealt with, the argument was raised that the concept of group, and indeed race, was itself nonsense. There was no such thing as a pure race and therefore a biological group. True, but irrelevant. People self-identify according to racial groups and these groups express generalized characteristics which the science is now teaching us has in many cases a solid biological basis.[5] It is in any case a strange argument, given that many of the critics of the research are from the Left and ardent supporters of affirmative action programmes which are based on….. well, race.

With that debate resolved, the next proposal was to decouple IQ scores and intelligence. Because a group had a comparatively lower average national IQ score than another group was not proof that they were less intelligent, just that they had a lower IQ score, which is not unlike saying that just because a medical thermometer gives you a reading of 104 deg C does not necessarily mean that you have a temperature. Quite what purpose IQ scores serve if they do not ultimately measure intelligence, remains unanswered.

Latest argument to explain why some societies succeed while other do not without mentioning the dreaded "G" word has been to attribute everything to the luck of the geographical lottery. Thus societies fortunate to find themselves in the most beneficial climatic and geographical regions thrived while others did not. Such arguments, of course, signally fail to explain *why* it was that some societies could identify opportunity and rise to it while others, sitting atop even better opportunities, failed to spot them. Again, it does not answer why some societies ended up in Gardens of Eden while others were driven to the climatic extremities. Lastly, of course, it cannot explain why even those societies which have the misfortune of living in less accommodating environments have still failed to adapt their social, farming, technological and economic organisations to create success --- despite all the examples that have gone before them.

By such ducking and diving did otherwise perfectly intelligent and insightful people try to avoid the inevitability of confronting the uncomfortable fact that if genes and biology influence the capabilities and characters of individuals at the micro level, they must certainly influence the characteristics of societies at the macro level. The balance of scientific evidence now suggests that the genetic contribution to the difference in IQ between individuals is 50% and between societies as much as 80%. But suggest that for open debate, and the roof caves in.

Again, few people dispute differences in physical appearances between groups brought about by the nature of their climatic exposure through the ages.[6] Yet suggest differences in the human brain, after all merely another organism of the body, and like a tickey in a jukebox, stand by for the same old name-calling rock-'n-roll from the Left.

It is so much politically easier to claim that differences between groups are "cultural" and to paternalistically suggest that with the right sort of interventions they can be smoothed away overnight. This Essay argues that what we call culture is no more than the social, political and economic manifestation of greater underlying forces, primarily genetic and only secondarily environmental. Emotionally to deny any genetic and biological influence in causing this difference between humans, is to indulge a dangerous fantasy. To keep hammering away at the things that are self-evidently common between us while ignoring or even denying factors which contribute to our difference, visible, patent and demonstrable difference, is dangerous, as politicians across the western world are now learning to their cost.

For six decades, the supporters of the Egalitarian Fantasy, have sought to deny the empirical and scientific evidence, in many cases mounting emotional and political challenges rather than technical objections and attacking the proponents of a material role for genes and biology in human formation as determinists, racists, new conservatives, troglodytes and even Nazis.

Yet the science continues to throw up overwhelming evidence of material differences in attitudes between racial, gender and ethnic groups in all sorts of ways: from composite intelligence levels, to the capacity for perseverance, to the quality of empathy, to attitudes towards punishment, to the levels of inter-personal trust, to the proclivity towards violence, to the levels of altruism beyond immediate kinship, to a predisposition to success or failure in life or nationhood [7]

Science writer Nicholas Wade in his ground-breaking *A Troublesome Inheritance: Genes, Race and Human History (2014),*[8] presents the compelling argument that the major races on earth have developed in continental separation for eons and it is therefore neither outrageous nor insulting to observe that races may have reached different genetic outcomes during this period, given the fact that science indicates that at least 14% of present genetic configurations in humans have evolved in the most recent past, 5 000 to 30 000 years, a blink of the eye in the history of humanity. To suggest that somehow humans reached perfect and immutable evolution at some distant past point is scientifically unsustainable. It is the stuff of real Flat Earthism. The tide of scientific evidence has thus been running heavily against the Egalitarian Fantasists in recent decades.

Those of us outside this bitterly fought contest between the experts, regard all this somewhat bemusedly. We can deduce from studies that there are differences between groups. We intuit this may well be tied up with genes and biology. No simpler example illustrates this vexed question than a reference to the published scale of average national intelligences of 108 nations. At the top with scores of 107 lie Singaporeans and South Koreans.

Other research puts Ashkenazi Jews at the very top at 108 and Australian Aboriginals at the bottom with 64. No serious person could suggest that the difference in average intelligence and socio-economic status is unconnected, or that genes and biology play no role in this difference, or that they can be wished or swished away by some light social interventions. So why this decades-long *omerta* on the issue?

Let it be said now: there is no grand conspiracy by the supporters of the Egalitarian Fantasy, no council of Fantasists or a Fantasist Fuehrer. There does not need to be. Wrapped in their cocoon of self-reinforcing belief, the Fantasists orbit with ever greater centrifugal force, drifting further and further from a reality experienced by the rest of us. They do not act in concert: they are individuals who constitute a significant slice of the Western elite pursuing the same goals through a mixture of widely shared ideology and self-interest.

What binds them is not conspiracy but what psychologist Irving L. Janis called Groupthink: a unifying set of beliefs which are endlessly internally reinforced by like-minded people and which demonises anybody who holds an opposing viewpoint.

Measure these few snatched quotations below from the revised edition of Janis's 1972 book, *Victims of Groupthink:*

A Psychological Study of Foreign-Policy Decisions and Fiasco's, against the way the Egalitarian Fantasists, have sought to deny and even repress the arguments of those striving for an understanding of the material role genes and biology play in the lives of individuals and nations.

"Groupthink is a mode of thinking that people engage in when they are deeply involved in a cohesive in-group, when the members' strivings for unanimity override their motivation to realistically appraise alternative courses of action.

"Groupthink refers to a deterioration of mental efficiency, reality testing, and moral judgement that results from in-group pressures.

"According to the Groupthink hypothesis, members of any small cohesive group tend to maintain esprit de corps by unconsciously developing a number of shared illusions and related norms that interfere with critical thinking and reality testing.

"One of the symptoms of Groupthink is the members' persistence in conveying to each other the cliché and over-simplified images of political enemies embodied in long-standing ideological stereotypes.

"... the alacrity with which members of a cohesive in-group suppress deviational points of view by putting social

> *pressure on any member who begins to express a view that*
> *deviates from the dominant belief of the group."*[9]

This Essay will argue that the dominant elites in the developed world have been so captured by Groupthink that
they have become unwilling to accept the major scientific
and empirical realities which have arisen to challenge their
Egalitarian Fantasy and its multitude of franchises, from
liturgical forms of human rights to extremist feminism to
zealot environmentalism to unconditional welfarism to
moralistic foreign interventionism. That, I suggest, lies at
the heart of the break-down of Western institutional integrity and the yawning gap in trust between those who
purport to lead and those who are supposed to follow.

The apogee of this denial was surely the publication
in 1984 of *Not in Our Genes* and the manifesto *Against
Sociobiology,* a riposte to Edward O Wilson's *Sociobiology:
The New Synthesis.* Wilson's work, published in 1975,
defined Sociobiology as "the systematic study of the biological basis of all social behaviour" and sought to explain
through an exhaustive study of huge numbers of different
species, the impact that biology has had through eons on
social behaviour and formations in man and beast.

Against Socio Biology was a semi-hysterical attack by a
Boston-based radical group called the Sociobiology Study
Group of Science for the People. It vehemently opposed

the very notion that there could be something called "human nature". The authors were mostly part of a so-called Radical Science Movement which mounted extreme and often violently offensive attacks against anybody in any field of science who attributed salience to genetic or biological heritability in the formation of human nature.

Not In Our Genes, by R C Lewontin, Steven Rose and Leon J. Kamin, was a project in which the authors, against the mounting evidence, denied genetics any material relevance in human intelligence, behaviour or success. Thus: "We assert that we cannot think of any significant human social behaviour that is built into our genes in such a way that it cannot be modified and shaped by social conditioning"[10]

Decrying the biological determinists as political poseurs serving the interests of the New Right represented by Margaret Thatcher and Ronald Reagan, the critics regrettably lent themselves to an even higher level of political spin in challenging the notion of genetic or biological determinism. Reading today the full blast of emotional rhetoric with which the authors attack their foes, one cannot but again be reminded of how historically exposed becomes an ideologically driven expert crazed by his or her own certainty.

Most of these debates raged in the late 1970's and through the 1980's. It is impossible to read them nearly half a century on without being impressed by the enormous ground that has since been covered in the neuro- and genetic-sciences, particularly in the wake of the epic Human Genome Project which was completed in 2003 and which mapped 23 000 human DNA elements influenced by genes.

This vast project brought a greater understanding of the nature of human organisms but ironically also brought more complexity. It really was not as simple as saying this gene does that this way and then that happens. In fact, it now appears that the difference arises not so much in genes as in the frequency with which alleles, a form of gene, occur, in an individual or group. Since 2003, legions of geneticists have been skilfully unpeeling this intriguing and beautiful fruit.

The advances made in medical genetic studies in understanding the origins of dread diseases and illnesses understandably grabs most of the headlines but behind that stands a wealth of work which has greatly improved our understanding of how genes drive human capacity and behaviour, whether for the better or the worse, and how the frequency of alleles craft the differences between us.

Only now can we appreciate how many blank holes have been filled in; how many once passionately waged arguments of the '70's ands 80's transpire to be quibbles

easily settled by the relentless advance of genetic research, and how many self evident truths have since been
eclipsed. It is as if those of us who reject the behaviourists
of the 70s are watching people attempting to grasp the
concept of 21st Century Smart Phone technology using
1970's terrestrial telephony ideas. One feels rather like a
member in the audience of a traditional English Christmas
Pantomime wanting to shout out to the hero: "Behind
you. Look behind you."

- But, inevitably, the science has forced the Fantasists
  to confront four deeply uncomfortable realities:
- The first is the reality that we are inherently
  different and indeed not all equal in our competence, aptitudes and capabilities[11], not just as
  individuals but as groups[12], not just in terms of
  our cognitive abilities as measured by a correlation of various IQ tests[13] but also in our non-
  cognitive abilities, best described as character
  traits.[14]
- The second reality is that the brains of men and
  women are neurologically differently wired thus
  ensuring measurable variances in aptitudes and attributes. This has social, political and economic
  import.[15]
- The third reality is that there are such things as
  innately successful individuals and groups and
  innately less successful individuals and groups,

and they tend to replicate from generation to generation.[16]
- Lastly is the reality that genetically embedded non-cognitive traits are vital to human success, or lack of it.[17]

Crucially, a profound swing is underway in our understanding of the human brain. Far from our minds being only software that can be reprogrammed by social engineers to create "success" or conformity, as generations of handsomely enriched behaviourists and social analysts have convinced us, it is in fact substantially a question of hardware.[18] This hardware consists of the chemicals in the human brain, the balance of those chemicals, the conformation of the pre-frontal cortex of our brains, the linkages between the brain's hemispheres and the ratios of fibre to "grey matter",[19].

Research undertaken at the Massachusetts Institute of Technology in the United States, thanks to the huge improvements in brain neuro imaging technology, can now pinpoint the neuro markers, the physical street signs, which indicate with great precision the character and potential capacity of individuals. Indeed, latest research indicates that scanning of the contours of the human brain is more effective by far in determining future prospects for, say, dyslexic people to mitigate their condition than conventional IQ or learning ability tests.

It is thus the structure of our DNA and the physical conformation of our brains that helps determine the attributes of individuals and groups, including their predisposition towards success or failure. Our new understanding of our sub-conscious is also changing old myths. Rather than it being a morass of inchoate images, buried memories and lost experiences, it is in fact a pretty smoothly functioning machine for sorting out the important information needed for our survival and success.[20] Many of the working parts of that machine were tooled even before we were born. Indeed, evolutionary anthropologists and psychologists argue these processes are derived from the biological character of our long dead ancestors.[21]

The Australian writer Christine Keneally, in her intriguing book, *The Invisible History of the Human Race*, published in 2014,[22] traces the close correlation between genealogy and genetics in the history of our species. She refers to the work done by modern geneticists at Oxford University using contemporary genomes to create maps of genetic pools which, when overlaid with what we know of the ancient world, correlate perfectly, thus revealing the enduring imprint of our respective gene pools through millennia.

Just one example: the genomic samples taken from rural British communities which had been long resident threw up, amongst others, distinctive genetic footprints in south-western England, western Scotland, Northern Ireland and north central England. Overlaid on what we know to be the map of immediate post-Roman Britain, they exactly cover the regions known to the Romans as Dalradia (Ulster and the West Scottish Coast), Reged (Cumbria), the Britonic Kingdom of Elmet (north central England) and Dumnonia (Cornwall).

Overlay the same genetic/tribal maps on a contemporary map showing the incidence of poverty in the UK provided by the European Commission in 2014 and, voila, the coincidence of boundaries, although by no means perfect, is remarkable. How can we not speculate about the rich interplay of genetic, biological, historical, political, economic, cultural and social processes whereby the genetic pools least influenced by the Romano-British presence and subsequent invasions, end up amongst the poorest regions of Britain two millennia later?

Then there is the importance of human general intelligence, also known as the g factor. This refers to the ability of humans to think, reason, anticipate, organise and solve problems. This potent element in the success or failure of an individual is measurable, largely genetic and heritable. It is also unequally dispersed between individuals and groups on class, race and national lines.[23]

Intelligence is not the *only* predicator of success but the whole range of hard and soft sciences are now telling us that there is indeed a "package" of cognitive and non-cognitive attributes in individuals and groups which are genetically and biologically derived. Some of those packages are "success packages" which predispose its holders to success in life and some are "failure packages" which point to the reverse. Again, the vital word is *predispose*, not *predetermine*. There is still leeway for environmental influences to make an impact on the fortunes of individuals and groups.

It thus serves no point to rail against pre-determinism simply because researchers are painstakingly building a case for the centrality of genetics and biology in human nature. To the extent that this can be considered "pre-determination", that is in any case not decided by the researchers who detect it, but by an infinitely greater force that made each and every one of us, what Matt Ridley cheekily calls the Genome Ordering Device or GOD.[24] One need not be judgmental or condescending about this, any more than when one considers the relative value of a Shire horse or a Thoroughbred, both magnificent creatures, both worthy of respect.

Imagine what human history would look like if we had bred Shires to carry the post and Thoroughbreds to plough the fields, all because we were too burdened by political correctness or too lazy to determine the best attributes granted to them by their package of genes. One can go on from there to make out a case that no matter the package, value in human and economic terms is still there to be attached. But what one cannot do is ignore the fact that there *are* such packages and they to a significant extent point to different life outcomes, a fact that fatally punctures the Fantasist's more extreme egalitarian arguments.

To have even suggested ten years ago that there could be a genetic or innate basis to differences in cognitive and non-cognitive ability between individuals, genders and groups would have led to an explosion of righteous indignation from the Fantasists --- and worse. Let us not forget that 30 years ago scientists were losing their tenured professorships at American universities and being hounded off campuses by foaming left-wing protestors for saying no more than what is today accepted as fact.[25]

Mercifully, that nonsense is all but over in its scientific sense but sadly not entirely in an academic or political one. The end of what one analyst called The Blank Slate Theory,[26] the belief that human abilities are formed almost entirely by environmental influence, may well have been the eclipse of the scientific basis of the Connectionist and the denting of the more extreme fringes of the Plasticist schools of thinking. These either attributed super human abilities to the human brain for its ability to adapt to environments, seemingly independent of genetic or innate influence, or sought to diminish the importance of genetic and biological heritability.

There are rear-guard actions, to be sure. Hillary and Steven Rose, arch opponents of the determinists and veterans of the early wars, published their *Genes, Cells and Brains* in 2014 when much water had flowed under the bridge. Intriguingly, the book had little to do with its title; the science was by then too settled so the authors segued from battling the content of the genomic sciences to decrying its context. The work is a full-blooded Leftist attack on genomic and bio-medical science itself: corporatist, capitalist, dominated by Big Pharma (the pharmaceutical industry), unethical, reracialising society, arrogant and divisive. If anything, the book was the sharp squeal of a departing idea, one that had reached sell-by date.

The debate has shifted significantly forward. We are getting beyond ideological disputes about whether there are innate differences between individuals, genders and groups. There is increasing evidence that different groups, classes, races and nations replicate these differences *in a generalized way,* although we are still a long way from a universal acceptance of the proposition. Increasingly, however, the focus now is on the *nature* and *cause* of those differences.

To what exact extent is this "hardware" infrastructure genetically embedded and inherited? How precisely does this contribute to the characteristics of humans? The current consensus is about half from heritable genes and the rest from external influences, minimally in the home environment and more extensively through experiences outside the home.[27] An exemplar of this work is the research published in 2014 by Sweden's Karolingska Institute which determined the enormous importance of genes in the formation of musical talent in the individual.[28] Again, the role of genetic and biological inheritance in sporting virtuosity has been variously confirmed by research[29]

But to what extent do inherited genes dictate the way in which individuals create their own environments? We know that the power of genetic heritability increases as one grows older. This is because one's genetic predisposition tends to create environments in which the individual is most comfortable, in which his or her genetic template is best reinforced.[30]

For example, the person born with the inherited genetic predisposition towards becoming a long distance Olympic runner will create an environment in which he or she can move towards that goal by joining the athletics team or pushing their aerobic fitness endurance or seeking out mentors or watching television sports programmes about athletics. It is called playing to the strengths of one's genotype and is often unwitting. It obviously implies an even greater debt to genetic heritability than suggested merely by direct genetic impact.[31]

Whether a person with these innate qualities *does* become an Olympic long distance runner, depends on a whole range of other factors which may be broadly called the optional extras or chance factors: the availability of role models, training facilities, sponsorships, quality of the competitors and even the timing of the Olympic year relative to the stage of development of the athlete.

The important point here is that while somebody with the genetic and biological propensity to become an Olympic long distance runner *might* get to the Olympics, somebody without those propensities most certainly will not. This is not a chicken or the egg riddle. It is the genes than come first, the environment second. The secret is in discerning as early as possible the former from the latter and not assuming that everybody has the innate capacity to get to the Olympics.

Extrapolation of findings by Toronto's York University in Canada suggest that there are only 100 000 naturally fit people in the United States, in other words genetically predisposed to Olympian Status, out of a population of 322 million. One instantly grasps how pointless it is to work on the assumption that everybody can be an Olympic athlete and accordingly invest huge amounts of time, energy and money in making it a reality. Yet that has pretty much been the basis of the Post-Modern social consensus in all areas of our life. It is the presumption on which we have built our modern social, political and economic orders and it is the foundation of the Egalitarian Fantasy.

Again, what importance do we assign to the influence of the more opaque process of epigenetics whereby changes are made to the neurons of the brain without affecting the individual's basic DNA structure?[32] A body of research suggests that mothers (latest research suggests also fathers)[33] affected by adverse circumstances like famine, stress, abuse or disease result in impairment of the daughter cells in a foetus with consequences for the behaviour and abilities of the off-spring.[34]

The research shows that nations with a high disease burden display a correspondingly low level of average national intelligence. The correlation is precise and points to the effects disease and stress through generations have on general national intelligence levels.[35] The science is also now determining the role that, for example, parental smoking has on the incidence of asthma in as yet unborn children[36], how obesity is transferred from mother to child through epigenetic processes[37] or how parental stress impairs the working memory capacity and thus executive function of children born to poor families.[38]

These outcomes occur due to the chemical process of methyllation whereby components of the daughter cells are impaired through the realignment of chemical atoms, causing damage to the important stress mitigators in the pre-frontal cortex of the brain, the engine house of the human mind. The net effect, the evidence suggests, is to create individuals of insecure, volatile, aggressive and impetuous natures with generally lower intelligence and inclined to substance abuse: in short, a predisposition, re-peat, not predestination, towards a life of failure.[39]

What is not known, however, is whether such epi-genetic change is reversible once the causes of stress are removed.[40] Are epigenetic characteristics as embedded as genetic ones? Are they in fact the same thing? How many generations of disease and stress free living, for example, obliterates the impact epigenetic change has wrought on average national intelligence in certain parts of the world?[41] Or will it lead to an increase in the number of promoter alleles in the MAO-A gene so as to reduce the dispropor-tionate representation of some minorities in the violent crime statistics of developed world countries?[42] The ques-tions are vital. If the burden of our genetic make-up, our genotype, is largely embedded and inherited, there is not that much that social interventions can do.

There is not yet much appetite for genetic modification of human cells to change our character, let alone the character of a whole group, although the tools to do it are available and it may yet come.[43] After all, if we can "genetically edit" foodstuffs, clone sheep, genetically eliminate dread ailments in embryonic form, change the genes of potential suicides before they are born, predict through DNA scanning whether a five year old child will be obese at 14, isolate gene KL-VS, the most important genetic agent of non-pathological variation in intelligence, thus opening the possibility of us eventually being able to pop a pill to be brighter, if all of this is now within our grasp or on a looming horizon, how long can it be before we can remake humans at the embryonic stage from being less successful to being successful to being mega-successful?

Rita Carter, in her book (1998) described the way in which the architecture and function of the brain might be modified to serve us better than the one derived from evolution. Drugs were the beginning but then, Carter presciently wrote, will come genetic engineering. "The system that once served us so well is encoded in our genes and by the dawn of the 21st century we will probably have the knowledge and techniques to tweak those genes to produce a brain that is better suited to its time."

This may sound like Science Fiction but as we all know, Sci Fi more often than not has proved to be real science delivered with fanfare by advance instalment. The only thing currently preventing the whole-sale genetic editing of human individuals and groups so as to make them brighter, stronger, healthier and less violent is a lack of resources, huge moral contention and the opposition of those who have a vested interest in keeping things just as they are.

This Essay does not presume to stray into an argument about the benefits of genetic editing to improve the human genetic stock. It will, however, make a different point. Let us use the tools we have to enhance our capacity to identify latent genetic talent in whatever field it may lie and from whatever background it may come and then grow that to its maximum potential.

In the absence of any broad consensus on mass human genetic editing, we thus turn to other options. If, one can make a case that much of our character is the result of epigenetic change caused by adverse pre-natal or even immediate post-natal experience, then we do not have to think of genetic modifications to improve people's life chances or prospects.

The argument in favour of social interventions at an early childhood stage has seized virtually the entire western political and pedagogical elite, given the absence of any good ideas immediately preceding it. Huge national resources are being deployed to this cause. Evidence of its success is still patchy, to say the least. One of the flagship projects, The Knowledge is Power Project in New York did indeed achieve remarkable High School grades amongst the target group from poor families, largely through huge financial and time investments in each child. Sadly, when the target group reached College and the support was withdrawn, the drop-out rate was scarcely better than the control group. Yet, it is on the still tenuous premise of massive early childhood intervention that the legions of bureaucrats in the educational "transformative" and social development arena now pin their hopes.[44]

But there is hope. Aggregate cognitive intelligence as measured by IQ, did indeed rise during the decades immediately after the Second World War for all groups. Its consequence has been most obvious in the equalising of IQ levels between males and females in the developed world as women increasingly engaged in the processes of modernity.[45] The impact is not as discernible in the developing world; indeed, the fastest rate of improvement in female IQ has been in the highest per capita GDP countries, indicating again the link between innate national human genetic capacity and national success.[46]

It has also narrowed the gaps in cognitive ability as measured by standard IQ tests between racial groups, although the latest evidence indicates this has now stabilised and a caution needs to be attached: other sub tests of the IQ score measuring other criteria for intelligence indicate little progress has been made in reducing the gaps between groups.[47]

But quite apart from the complexities of IQ measurement, lies another factor. The sheer challenge of migrating from one social class to another adds significant stress levels which, the evidence suggests, some groups are better at managing than others. Research in the US on a sample from the minorities who had migrated from the underclass to the middle class, for example, revealed the fact that these enterprising individuals had incurred disproportionate allostatic loads (stress in simple terms) in making the journey, with potentially damaging impact on their future physical and mental well being.[48] The research suggests that the impact of social migration is not equally felt between individuals and groups.

Whichever way one chooses to look at it, the science is challenging some of the fundamental assumptions of the post modern world. If success, or lack of it, is at root a "hardware" problem and not a "software" one, the prospects for changing an individual or group's chances of success merely by social engineering are surely constrained. If we are unequally equipped to take advantage of equal opportunity, how can we expect equal outcomes? If we accept that intelligence is a major predicator to future success in life, why do we insist on ignoring its salience?

Again, if we accept that the negative effects of epigenetic change may be generational or even multi-generational, why pretend we can sort the problem with a few quick-fix social interventions? Why keep blaming successful people for skewering the system against unsuccessful ones when lack of success is primarily a genetic or epigenetic condition, not a social one. Or unfairly castigating unsuccessful people and groups for not achieving objectives imposed upon them that are not attainable? Why keep banging on about the centrality of "culture" in determining human behaviour when it is all largely in the chemicals and "culture" is in fact no more than the social, political, artistic and economic expression of individual and collective genotypes ? And, more to the point, what is the sense in promoting the premise that we can all be equal if only enough money is spent?

One cannot blame the leaders of 1945 for being unaware of all this. They just did not know better. But there is no excuse for anybody to deny it now. In fact, the flawed assumptions on which the Egalitarian Fantasy has been constructed have been evident for at least the last two decades but have been concealed by widely differing yet powerful intellectual, emotional and financial interests.

First, conservatives and religious bodies in the developed world saw any suggestion of an innate human nature as threatening to the notion of free will because without free choice there can be no such thing as good and evil, human sin, repentance and redemption.

Second, the Left believed that we were no more than the sum of the social influences to which we are subjected during our life. To suggest otherwise, was to diminish the role of social engineering; the bedrock of all totalitarian, communist, socialist and welfare systems.

Third, many people believed that by merely referring to difference between groups, would open society up to racism, anti-Semitism, tribalism and sectarianism. This belief, perhaps understandably, was often most fiercely held by people of Jewish extraction, many of them individuals who were extremely influential in academia in the decades after the war, particularly in the behaviourist and educational fields.

Fourth, the concept of irreducible national success deficits constituted a major threat to the solicitation of aid by poor and mendicant countries. If social interventions were of little use, why should rich countries continue with aid programmes, was the concern.

Fifth, the very basis of the developed world's consumer society was to persuade people that they could be anything they wanted to be, if only they used the right hair shampoo/underarm deodorant/cars/mobile phones/app. The notion that people cannot be everything they want to be was just plain bad business.

Finally, as the leftist world view began to assume overwhelming dominance amongst the post World War ll elites, vast and entrenched bureaucracies sprung up, particularly in the educational, advocacy and "caring" fields, whose very existence depended on a continuation of the belief that humans were infinitely malleable in the creation of utopian and egalitarian societies --- just as long as good money was thrown at the problem.

All of these protagonists of Fantasy were misguided. Granting genetic and biological forces their rightful role in the formation of individuals and groups, strengthens, rather than weakens, the inherent value of human difference. Humans can still be held accountable for their actions; can still be expected to perform to the moral expectations of their community. The *recognition* of certain genetically and biologically driven negative characteristics does not automatically imply *condoning* them.

Social interventions can still play a part in helping people develop to the maximum of their genetic and biological potential. Merely suggesting that we are innately different with different aptitudes is not a short cut to the death camps: the reverse. By identifying those differences we can help individuals play to the strongest element of their genotype as rapidly as possible --- to their benefit and that of the society. What can be wrong with that?

Indeed, research by John Hopkins University in Maryland published in 2014 points to the discovery of a gene, SKA 2, which predisposes individuals to suicide.[49] Modified to normalize the presence of cortisol and suddenly the risk of suicide during a person's life are dramatically reduced. If we can consider "editing" people genetically to prevent them from taking their life at some future point, why can we not use the same body of science to help guide people rapidly towards their optimum genetic capability to enhance their life's chances?

The suppression of discussion of differences between groups by modern elites in fact says much about their own insecurities. There are innumerable examples of people of diverse communities working together even under very adverse conditions, as long as they are left to get on with it. It is when vested interests seek to appropriate political or economic gain from difference, or its denial, do the problems arise.

Worse, by refusing to acknowledge the salience of visible differences between groups, indeed by actively suppressing discussion of it, the elites merely cut sticks to beat their own backs. The resurgence of right of centre forces in European, and that includes British politics, around the issue of mass immigration precisely makes the point.

It is easy to dismiss all of this as an intellectual or philosophical debate best left to the egg heads and moralists; a dreary repetition of the age-old nurture versus nature argument. It is not that simple. We are at last facing up to the realisation that high level human genetic capability may be globally finite and in fact diminishing as a proportion of the overall genetic capacity of the species, precisely as the demand for that commodity is soaring in a globalised and technologically advancing world.

Yet even as new scientific evidence tumbles out on a virtual weekly basis about our fundamental nature as humans, the elites prove incapable of making the intellectually courageous leap required to ask the simple question: so what does all this mean for our social, political and economic formations? One does not require great imagination to grasp that an entire order based on a scientific fantasy cannot have durability.[50] It has so proven in lost economic competitiveness, failed welfare states, flailing state institutions and huge social confusion. The immediate consequence of the Egalitarian Fantasy has been to disconnect ordinary human beings from the things that give content to their lives --- Faith, family, nation, loyalty, work. They are thus made more malleable units in the creation of the Left's utopian and totalitarian institutions;

the socialist, nanny, welfare state. In this they have been spectacularly successful in the developed world.

And it is not enough simply to destroy people's present sense of themselves: it is essential to obliterate their identification with the past for that too gives humans a sense of place, continuity, resilience and self-assuredness --- all things loathed by the Left. Hence the dislike of the Egalitarian Fantasists for genealogical inquiry and the work geneticists are doing to build the link between our individual pasts and our present.

The end of the Cold War in the early 1990's provided the developed world with a rare opportunity to define the 21st century as one of advantage for itself and all others. What did we do with the gems of our newly acquired scientific knowledge about ourselves and our social formations? What did we do with our stewardship of a unipolar world when we could have really made the difference in establishing a reasonably fair and stable world?

We fell back on the same old Egalitarian Fantasy that had been driving our thinking for decades. Instead of massively investing the peace dividend in developing our human and physical infrastructure to a point of untouchability, we blew our national treasures on creating vast welfare systems and ineffectual public educational regimes that have yielded little more than ever greater inequality and dependency, all based on the false belief we are all equal in our ability to rise to opportunity.

Rather than seeking to build a world order based on stable and pro-Western developing world nations, irrespective of their systems of governance, our reckless interventions in pursuit of an egalitarian and moral imperialism have brought an arc of devastation from North Africa, through the Middle East to Eastern Europe. The legacy is more refugees than at any time since World War ll and a greater swathe of the globe's surface now without effective government since the late 19th century, outside World War.

Instead of building economically strong and competitive sovereign states co-operating only on absolutely core interests, in Europe we created a vast, intrusive, anti-democratic, uncompetitive and dysfunctional entity with a failed common currency at its heart, all of this based on the absurd notion that simply because countries share a geographic area they are the same and that they are equal. Here too is only pitiful waste and lost opportunity.

In short, the Egalitarian Fantasy has brought the developed world to the brink of historic irrelevance. It has made its economies uncompetitive, its societies confused and aggrieved, its politics both intrusive and pointless, its military prowess questionable, its international status risible and its prospects uncertain. In sixty years it has, quite literally, brought us to what might prove to be the closing era of a 500 year "Western Empire".

FIVE STAGES TO HISTORIC IRRELEVANCE

The preceding section of this essay has sought to record the disconnect that exists between the Western elites' perception of human nature and the reality as now affirmed by a surging science. This disconnect pervades every interstice of life in the developed world and has had grave consequences for public policies which have been built on what *ought* to be as opposed to what actually *is*. From being the dominant force in world affairs, the West has slipped into a state of stagnant economies, frozen international conflict and fractured internal politics. I define the term "West" not so much from its geo-location but more as shorthand for the grouping of mainly northern hemisphere nations with a core belief in democracy as that term is widely understood.

This section of the Essay will consider how it all happened and within living memory. The five post-war stages to the irrelevance of the developed world, thanks to The Egalitarian Fantasy, are simply told.:

- Stage One could be called the **Splash the Cash Project**.
- Stage Two was the **Downsizing To Mediocrity Process**.
- Stage Three was the **Jobs Exodus Moment**.
- Stage Four, the pivot, was the **Fantasy Work Cycle**.
- Stage Five, the final one, was the catastrophic **Debt For Wealth Drive**.

These are not water tight stages. In many cases they merge one into the other or run concurrently. But they do represent the seminal processes leading the developed world to its current impasse. Let us follow their doleful course.

In Stage One, Splash The Cash, developed world countries diverted unimaginable levels of national wealth in a fruitless effort to encourage the mass upward migration of poor individuals and groups, whether at home or abroad.[1] More, they created pension liabilities of extraordinary generosity relative to available resources. Each regime of populist politician exceeded the preceding one in offering ever increased levels of benefit. Critical investments in infrastructure --- both human and physical --- played second fiddle to deploying resources in the social support of unproductive human assets, whether working age unemployed or pensioners.[2]

But after forty years, nearly two generations, it was apparent that the investment was a failure in countries like the United Kingdom and the United States.

Social distance and income inequality had grown, not decreased.[3] The rate of upward mobility of the lowest quintile to a higher quintile had remained for generations as it had always been: roughly one in ten within a single generation, no different to the proportion of rank-and-file British soldiers who in 1862 seized the army's offer of free literacy and numeracy training to progress through the ranks.[4] The rate of social mobility in the United States was of almost exactly the same order: about nine per cent of the bottom quintile of the population would make a higher quintile in a generation.[5]

Nothing had changed this 10% quota of "strivers" or "aspirers" from the lower groups; not the growth of general prosperity, the advent of mass secondary school education, the franchise or the deployment of chunks of national wealth to advance the poor. Then, some twenty years ago, coinciding with the first effects of The Egalitarian Fantasy, even this limited mobility staggered to a halt in developed world countries.[6] Indeed, some research would suggest that the rate of social migration today is less than in Medieval times.[7] The project had foundered on the rocks of genetic limitation.

Stage Two, Downsizing To Mediocrity, saw the response of the Egalitarian Fantasy to the stubborn immobility of the left behind people in their societies. If they could not be persuaded to advance on a broad front, everyone else must be slowed down to close the gap. This was called ''social justice" and its main proponents were the socialists and welfarists and their numerous ideological fellow travellers in the "caring", "transformative", "charity" and "victim" industries. It had four components.

In the first, public education systems were dumbed-down to accommodate the slowest. International competitive league tables showed this sudden fall in standards in the hard subjects of science and math, particularly in the Anglo Saxon countries, measured against the newcomers.[8] Grade inflation reached absurd proportions.[9] The catastrophe of "mixed ability" teaching, whereby advanced and regressed pupils were dumped together in the hope the laggards would be pulled up by the others, had the reverse effect. The frontrunners were pulled down.[10]

The foremost instrument for this devaluation of educational currency by the Egalitarian Fantasists in the educational establishment was the substitution of knowledge-based education requiring higher levels of cognitive capacity with experience-based or outcomes-based education, with all its derivatives such as problem-solving, ways of thinking, team responses and so on, none of which in practice demanded any particular level of cognitive capacity at all and although great fun, involved hardly any knowledge transfer.

The effect of this change was best seen in the UK. From being fourth in the OECD's Programme for International Student Assessment (Pisa) in science in 2000 it had dropped to 21st by 2012. From seventh in reading it had tumbled to 23rd. From eighth in math it had fallen to 26th. Research by the OECD in 2014, meanwhile, revealed the disconcerting fact that children in EU countries were receiving no better education than their grandparents and in the UK's case, even worse. British teachers, it found, worked longer hours than their European counterparts but the educational output was worse. Why? The teachers' time was swallowed up by endless and repetitive creation of work sheets and study projects rather than concentrating on teaching off established and long-standing texts.[11]

The resource that had once been Britain's greatest strength, the quality of its educators, had been diminished, not because of any lack of care or commitment on the part of the broad mass of the teaching corps, but by the huge diversions imposed on them by the Egalitarian

Fantasists, the bureaucrats and a gravely misdirected body of "transformative" educationists. In every case, those nations which *did* teach knowledge-based education were the winners.

Sports days at government schools in the UK meanwhile became "motor skills festivals" and any genuinely competitive events were banned for fear of creating an environment which might discourage the losers. The consequence: a tragic decline in the success of British team sports in international competitiveness while paradoxically significant achievement by individuals in athletics, golfing, swimming, cycling and club, but not national, football. Britain had stopped doing Team. It was over to the individual, a quarter from private educational backgrounds, to keep the flag flying. Nothing should be done to challenge the levelling project. An equality of mediocrity reigned in public education and on the playing fields of nations such as the UK.

This combination of deflated educational standards, inflated grades (inflated job descriptions too: electricians suddenly became "engineers" while town clerks transmogrified into "chief executive officers" with vastly inflated accompanying salaries and benefits) led to a shearing of a key link in successful countries: that between *qualification* and *competence.* This was the first warning light in the developed world's cockpit console.

The second response to the inability of the left behind groups to rise to abundant opportunity was a sustained and systematic assault by the Left on all remnants of what they called "elitism" that was in fact nothing but a drive to reduce the high knowledge, high value, wealth creating and wealth holding sectors of society to a quivering minority, wracked by a sense of guilt and self-abnegation for being successful. It was a project conceived in envy, born in spite and executed with unparalleled intellectual violence.

And it was hugely successful. Although only 11% of the UK population, for example, could objectively be defined by 2013 as working class by education, occupational status or socio-economic class, fully half of the population self-identified itself as "working class". Less than one per cent identified itself as "upper class". It was just too dangerous.[12]

If one needs to put a name and a date to the beginning of this onslaught it has to be the infamous document called *Studies in the Scope and Methods of the Authoritarian Personality*, a 1954 research project funded by the American Jewish Committee's Department of Scientific Research and chaired by a leading figure in the 1930's Frankfurt School of émigré German left-wing philosophers and thinkers.[13]

The intentions of the authors in attempting to get to grips with the infamy of the Nazi mind were no doubt entirely honourable. The effect, however, was pernicious.

The work sought to portray conservative or traditional values as aberrational and those espousing them as having the inherent qualities of F for Fascism. The holders of F tendencies were thus not merely misinformed but mentally unbalanced, suffering from some sort of personality disorder. The argument was gratefully appropriated by the Soviet Union which went the next logical step and declared that anybody opposed to its ideas was *ipso facto* insane and rightfully fit for incarceration in a mental institution.

In the years to come the import of the study would strike a mortal blow to the core conservative values of discipline, work, faith, loyalty, patriotism, tradition and family. The central premise of *The Authoritarian Personality* was seized upon by the Left and the numerous intellectual descendants of the Frankfurt School and they have never relinquished its seductive premise: that conservatism and traditionalism is not a political position but a personality disorder and that rational discussion with conservative opponents is impossible and unnecessary.

This thinking has pervaded all aspects of the postmodern world. Left-wing educationists, academics, lawyers, jurists, journalists, public servants, writers and film directors were the Revolutionary Guards driving the process. In so doing they became trapped by Groupthink, as described more fully above. With calculated ruthlessness they swept conservatives from positions of authority on western university campuses and purged major media organisations of anybody with right leaning sentiments.

The consequences are with us daily: people who oppose industrialised renewable energy are likened to Holocaust deniers or called Flat Earthers; parents who wish to give their children the best chance in life are "pushy" or, worse, saboteurs; people wishing to defend the value of their homes from intrusion by the profiteers of the green industry are termed NIMBY's; those who raise issues pertinent to a specific ethnic group are racist or fascist; those who call for a return to traditional and conservative values are "swivel-eyed loons" and those who resist the loss of national and cultural sovereignty to undemocratic and elitist multinational organisations are branded populist --- the last spat out with the deepest venom. It is of course intellectual fascism by another name.

Nothing captured this insulting dismissiveness better than the issue of mass immigration into the developed world. Those who opposed it were variously described by the elites as troglodytic, left-behind, right wing extremists, regressive, uncomprehending or manipulated. It did not occur to these elites that large numbers of thinking and educated people opposed mass migration because they had legitimate grounds for seeing it as a threat to their national values and way of life, a threat created merely to serve the interests of liturgical internationalists and the commercial imperative of big business for cheap and compliant labour.

But now a great irony was before us. The attempts by the Fantasists to portray their critics as deranged, had been turned by science. It was the Fantasists who were now accused of being unhinged. The "F" was no longer for Fascist, it was for Fantasist. It was they who had exhibited the classic, debilitating symptoms of Groupthink. It was they who had wrought an enduring and destructive impact on the developed world's future through the relentless pursuit of a scientific chimera, the Egalitarian Fantasy. This is what lies at the heart of the existential crisis now confronting the developed world.

But poor educational standards, meaningless bits of paper qualifications and a diet of vituperation against the "toffs" and conservatives, could not in itself make innately unsuccessful people earn more money or be more productive or themselves become "successful".

Thus arose the third component in the campaign to thrust this challenged group forward.

One element demanded that people should be employed not on evident competence or skill, but on *potential.* This roughly translated into a plethora of affirmative action and "diversity" projects. In some cases these initiatives succeeded in regard to individuals with the innate genetic competence to achieve, the ten percenters. But in many other cases it had no such happy outcome: the reverse. It was discovered belatedly that many people had limited potential --- mere race, gender or impoverished origin could not ensure it --- and the consequences were uniformly bleak in the further stereotyping of individuals and groups, the disillusionment of employers, the waste of resources and the creation of tension with peers not amongst the favoured group. We will pick up this theme later.

The last route to thrust this group forward was to artificially inflate the social cost of labour in an attempt to narrow the income gap between successful and unsuccessful groups. The quality of public benefit services was equalised, at enormous cost, irrespective of the contribution of the individual to the society or economy.[14] The gap between direct wages and what individuals actually derived through all the supplementary benefits, allowances, perquisites and services ballooned. From equivalence in 2000, the gap between wage and non-wage income in the developed world had grown to 17% by 2014. The link between the *price* of labour and the *value* of labour was snapped. A second warning light flashed on the cockpit console.[15]

THE FLIGHT OF REAL JOBS

All this ushered in Stage Three in the developed world's march to irrelevance, the Jobs Exodus Moment. This is a familiar modern tale. The high and ideologically inflated social cost of labour in developed countries, the collapse of mass educational standards, the attacks on wealth creators, all of it driven by the Egalitarian Fantasy, saw the relocation of capital to countries where educated, disciplined and cheaper labour was prepared to do the same tasks, only better and with infinitely less hassle.

This process was hastened in countries like the UK by the decision of successive governments to see the country's future as primarily knowledge and high skills based and to deconstruct its industrial component. This policy was based on the purest egalitarian fantasy: that all sections of the community were innately *capable* of serving a high knowledge economy and that all could benefit. It was only one of a huge number of mistakes made by the political elites, particularly those of the Left. At its heart was a fundamental misunderstanding of human nature, its potential and its genetic limitations.

With the flight of capital went jobs and entrepreneurs. It began with Japan in the 1970's and 1980's and moved to China, India, Bangladesh, Brazil, Turkey, Mexico and other places in the 1990's. In 2013, Price Waterhouse Cooper estimated the average monthly rate of wages in the developed world was still seven times higher than in China, despite Chinese wages having shown strong real growth for more than a decade.

Now, if ever, was the time for Western political leaders to speak truth to their publics, to tell them they would have to work harder, longer and better for less money, they would have to save more to ensure their lifestyles. Now, if ever, was the time for a frank conversation in which people would be told that one could not personally take out of a system more than one put back into it; that the expectations one had of life had to be aligned with one's own capacity to achieve them. Primarily, they should have made clear that individuals were responsible for their own destinies and that of their families. The State was only a last, desperate backstop.

They did not. If once the essence of democracy was that The People should not be afraid to speak Truth to Power, the travesty that is modern popular democracy determines that Power is too afraid to speak Truth to The People. And if it does, it is usually the last time it has the opportunity.

AND THE GROWTH OF FANTASY JOBS

Thus began Stage Four, the pivot, the Fantasy Job Cycle. Faced with declining real employment as a result of their Egalitarian Fantasy, developed world governments embarked on a massive deceit. They created *fantasy* jobs in the bureaucracies, in the quasi governmental organisations, in the multinationals and, most successfully, by sponsoring the exponential growth of what is called the charities or voluntary or non-profit or non governmental organisations. By rights it should be generically tagged the Neo Governmental sector, as its operational costs are in any case nearly 70% funded by public money.[1]

The sector does, however, have one huge benefit which public servant employees do not offer. The Neo Government bureaucrats are off book, thus camouflaging the real extent to which jobs are sponsored by public money.[2] It is, in short, an out-sourced, fantasy job creation project geared to hide the fact that real jobs have largely evaporated and that workers in the developed world are now subsidised by the state to a degree unmatched even by some of the dying communist regimes.[3]

The developed world's bureaucracies exploded with a new generation of proxy or fantasy jobs: assistant teachers who were not allowed to teach, police officers who could not affect an arrest, nurses who could not nurse except at the most basic level. The private sector matched this with a surge of jobs now demanded by the Egalitarian Fantasy: diversity officers, outreach personnel, armies of human resource operators, environmentalists, human rights lawyers, counsellors, a multiplicity of compliance officers to enforce the deluge of regulations, protocols and proscriptions. Britain's educational sector, exemplar of so many of the conceits of the Egalitarian Fantasy, is a case in point. In 2000, 75% of people employed in the sector were professional teachers, according to UK official statistics. By 2010 it was 53%, the rest consisting of administrative, ancillary, support and "intervention" personnel.

A casual canvas of the jobs pages of the UK publication, *The Guardian,* foremost mouthpiece of the jobsworthy industry, says everything that needs to be said about the generative power of the nonsense job sector.

All of this had to have its justifying mythologies and so this make-work was accompanied by tidal waves of mindless and meaningless bureaucratic rubbish. *Function* became subordinated to the need for *process* so that the box-ticking needed for passing a local government budget, for example, took more time than setting the budget itself. Preparing a "risk assessment" for a school outing took up more time than the trip. An iconic example: the London Metropolitan Police managed to produce a 400 page manual *on how to ride a bicycle.* It never ended as the voracious demand for fantasy jobs generated fantasy laws, generated fantasy functions.

Worse, bureaucrats became promoted not on the basis of how well they could manage issues or outcomes, the hall mark through history of successful statesmen, generals, public servants and business leaders, but on how well they could manage pointless and time-consuming processes. Business schools and consultants flourished, just as famed Western efficiency floundered.

Jobs were created not because of a demand for the services rendered but because of a demand for *jobs*, any ones and created by any means necessary. The growth of Big Government thus had little to do with creating essential services for the betterment of society, about meeting real needs. It was about replacing real jobs with fantasy ones --- and saving the politicians the embarrassment of explaining falling employment numbers.

And thus was born the greatest advocacy sector in the history of humankind, the Race, Misery, Gender, Guilt and Fear industries, or let us more crisply call it in the collective, supercrisis.org. These vast multi national corporations depended on two products: guilt and fear. These they imaginatively marketed to a terrified public through a variety of franchises.[4]

Great Scares have proved enduring and profitable through human history to politicians and businessmen alike; indeed institutions like stock markets are based on the skilled direction of what could be called artfully managed perpetual scare. No less the late 20th Century and 21st Century Great Scares: the millennium fear that

our computers would crash and leave our modern society devastated; the insistence that Aids would carry us all
to our early death; endless scares around "pandemic" exotic disease and lastly and most impressively, the Global
Warming Scare that promises us universal toasting un-
less we cripple our modern economies (adroitly retagged
"Climate Change" once it became apparent that the planet
was inconsiderately hardly warming at all). Two things
characterized these projects: vested interests taking profitable advantage of public gullibility and, second, they
were all based on a core of truth maliciously expanded
into a wealth of rent-seeking lies.

By the first decade of the 21st century supercrisis.org
had opened franchises in every sphere of human activity: security, health, environment, human rights, gender
rights, race issues, animal rights, domestic violence, "slavery" and so endlessly on. By such means did it extract the
money it needed to meet business plans, pay its wages,
secure its pensions and above all, qualify for the largesse
of the public purse.

This Essay does not argue that necessary and beneficial humanitarian work was not carried out by some
organisations. Or that others did not play a useful
role in identifying unfair practices in society. It certainly does not argue against the value of voluntarism
or seek to denigrate the selfless individuals who give

of their time freely and uncomplainingly to advance the interests of the less fortunate. Voluntarism is one of the bedrocks of successful, cohesive communities. What is at issue, however, is the way this voluntarism and the goodwill attached to it has been corporatized, globalised, politicised and turned into a job multiplier. What is opposed is the expansion of charitable "mission" for no other reason than to keep people in employment.

Once again it must be emphasised: this formidable enterprise should not be graced by the term conspiracy. It was not: merely millions of humans seized by Groupthink following the individual pursuit of financial rewards through common and concerted action.

Non-profit company revenues in the United States increased in real terms --- excluding the effect of inflation --- by 41% between 2000 and 2010. By 2014 it was earning $621bn in revenue and accounting for 5.5% of US gross national product. Incredibly, this was only slightly less than the contribution of the entire retail sector to US GDP.[5] In the UK, by 2014, there were 161 266 voluntary or charity organisations employing 1.9 m people full-time.[6] The entire local government sector managed to employ only 2.3 m. UK taxpayers gave nearly $20 billion to non-profit organisation, including charities, in 2014. Fifteen thousand people in the charities in the UK were earning in 2013 above $90 000 a year, more than twice the national average, 1 200 earned above $150 000 a year and 55 above $375 000.[7]

Oxfam, one of the titans of the industry and mentioned here purely for illustration, comprised seventeen divisions operating in 96 countries by 2014, employing 10 000 people and targeting an annual turn-over of $1.4 billion. Its 2013/14 annual report showed that 42% of its income came from public sources and a further 19% from trading, or more specifically, the operating of its charity shops competitively against severely disadvantaged small businesses. Nearly one third of its costs were for "non-programme" items. It just does not get more corporate than that.

This expansion in the costs and scale of the social services enterprise was largely unremarked, hidden under the broader rubric of the huge expansion of the services sector itself. This sector grew from being a contributor of half of GDP in 1980 to two thirds in 2013, according to World Bank statistics. There was a great irony here. As the numbers of people in formal government employment fell after the economic crisis of 2008, so precisely did the number of people employed in the neo government sector rise. In the UK alone, supercrisis.org employment jumped 40% between 2002 and 2012.[8]

This was simply a fantasy job reallocation programme but with a critical difference. While government employees were under nominal democratic control, the bureaucrats in the neo-governmental sector were not, even though they were more influential in shaping the public mind and, more insidiously, public policy via think tanks – the EU's Transparency Register now has around 6,000 entries, which makes up an estimated 75% of Brussels' business representatives and 60% of NGOs. The figure matches a rough number of 30,000 lobbyists in Brussels.

But the logic of huge industries based on the business of crisis demands, firstly, that crises can never be allowed to end and, secondly, that there must be an inexhaustible supply of "victims" to justify the employment of legions of people to act as carers/interlocutors/champions of these "victims". Inevitably, it was the lower classes mostly relegated to the job of victim and the middle classes who snapped up the jobs as promoters of the interests of the victims.

Thus began the continuous, draining process by which supercrisis.org reinvented itself by changing the definition of a crisis to ensure that it remained a crisis and that new battalions of "victims" could be thrust into service as the fodder for the advocacy industry. Across this vast industry, millions of people were employed not to resolve crises but to manufacture, expand and entrench them. Millions more were assigned the role of professional victim.

The examples are legion. Let us follow just a few.

THE POVERTY FRANCHISE

When massive improvements in the key UN living standards indicators were largely achieved throughout the
world --- almost entirely due to the efforts of China, a
country no longer afflicted by the Egalitarian Fantasy[1] ---
poverty data were quickly manipulated upwards to camouflage the fact that astonishing progress had been made
in alleviating world poverty. That simply did not fit with
the mythology. This was also done in developed world
countries. Since the advent of the welfare state, poverty
in its abject and historic sense has largely ceased to exist
as a reality for all citizens, apart from a truly fractional
minority of dysfunctional individuals who for whatever
reason choose to operate outside the welfare net or are
illegally resident in the country and barred from access
to welfare services. This confronted supercrisis.org with
a challenge. Poverty datum lines were graphed upwards
on the basis of computer modelling with little attempt to
define real and objective conditions of poverty as opposed
to a notional and computationally derived concept.[2]

An additional twist was the introduction of the idea of
"social exclusion" as a determiner of poverty. Taken to its

logical conclusion, where it will most certainly eventually be driven, it could mean that a child excluded from an expensive private school was a victim of poverty, or that a person refused entry to an exclusive club was impoverished. If this sounds like argument by absurdity, it should not. The inevitable end point of all Egalitarian Fantasies is the absurd.

By creating the concept of "social exclusion", the poverty franchise had brilliantly sidestepped the debate about real or existential poverty versus relative poverty. All poverty became relative. No longer was it important to determine objective levels of poverty in terms of cost of basic shelter, daily calorie requirements and clothing. Now one could measure poverty against an endlessly escalating tariff of lifestyle entitlement. It was a crisis-maker's dream.

Having created the notion of a poverty "crisis" in the developed world, supercrisis.org rushed in to fill it with franchises. Across the developed world, the concept of the "charity shop" became ubiquitous. These outlets, once populated by grey-haired volunteer retirees seeking to raise a few bucks for a favourite cause, became part of huge national and international retail chains, answering to regional and national offices, given turn-over targets and locked into skilful marketing campaigns.

When "austerity" became the watch word in the wake of the 2008 financial crisis, food banks surged to the fore. In some countries, the southern European periphery most affected by the devastation of the Egalitarian Fantasy of a common currency, for example, they served a purpose. In other countries like the UK, they were make-work projects and political sticks for opposition parties. Despite the most convincing evidence from a study of the numbers provided by the UK Office for National Statistics that there was no material "cost-of-living squeeze" on the broad range of households, in fact expenditure on recreation and leisure as a proportion of total household expenditure had *increased* during so-called austerity, supercrisis. org effortlessly managed to convince the broad public that there was a crisis and to give generously.

The consequences of all this make-work were of course baleful, not least because it increased an already pathological sense of dependency amongst the already substantial dependency classes, together with a sense of entitlement. But it also had economic consequences. The charity retail franchises, enjoying rates exemptions and tax free status, competed directly and unfairly with second hand shops and even speciality outlets, driving them out of business. Subsidised charity meals, offered without qualification to all comers, threatened lower-end private eateries and cafes and the food banks even began to eat into supermarket turnovers.[3] All of this led to unemployment, dependency and a demand for charity, which was of course the point.

Again, "homelessness" was redefined to refer to households in which a child had to share a bedroom with another child or a 19-year-old, perfectly capable of living with his or her parent, was deemed in need of a home. The quick out from living under the parental roof in countries like the UK became the conception of a child. Single parents took precedence on housing lists, thus creating another cascade of unintended consequences to be discussed later.

The twin sister of the "homeless" franchise was the "housing" franchise. By endlessly making the criteria for eligibility easier and working through other franchises to ensure a flow of impecunious immigrants, the franchise guaranteed that the housing "backlog" numbers kept growing, no matter how many homes were built or allowances extended. The welfare state of course ensured that many elderly people who would under normal circumstances have sold their homes to younger buyers before down-sizing to retirement places or smaller units, were able to hang on to their commodious homes, thus compounding the problem of housing availability.

This "need" for housing was so successful in countries like the UK that the state continued to bankroll the construction of new units although hundreds of thousands of unoccupied units were available (600 000 in the UK alone) and in countless cases housing authorities battled to find local people to fill this ostensibly aching need. In this project of course, one saw the finest example of self-serving triangulation between an Egalitarian franchise, business and local authorities to create and then fill a masterfully engineered "need".

THE HEALTH FRANCHISE

One of the richest fields of profit for supercrisis.org had to be health for the simple reason that it is the issue that can most easily engender fear in individuals and societies. The franchise operated multi-level. People were defined as "mentally ill" by changing the definitions[1] or, the old wheeze, creating new ones like Involutional Paranoia for the elderly[2] or promoting elusive ones like ME[3] or through declaring a "crisis" in the incidence of, osteoporosis and Alzheimer's, which are not crises at all but the simple arithmetic reality that if there are more old people as a proportion of a population who are living for longer, there will be more sufferers of these conditions.

Another example was the massive expansion of the definitions of post combat stress disorders for returning serviceman. So successful was the latter that by 2013, *half* the US servicemen returning from Iraq and Afghanistan were applying for medical disability payments even though less than four per cent actually saw a shot fired in anger.[+]

An intriguing battle broke out in 2013 between the authors of the Bible of psychological diagnosis, the *US Diagnostic and Statistical Manual of Mental Disorders* and a group called the Psychiatric Genomics Consortium which attempted to push the publishers to recognise in its fifth edition the role genetics and biology plays in psychological pathologies.

The detail does not concern us but what does emerge is the enlargement of the scope of psychiatric illness through the years to the point where the mildest form of depression, irritation, bad temper or lapse in self-discipline were now considered mental illness. None of this had anything to do with treating illness. It did, however, have everything to do with creating fantasy jobs.

Professor Chris Dowrick, Professor of Primary Medical Care, at Liverpool University, writing in the *British Medical Journal* in 2013 made the point that over-diagnosis of mental illness was now a bigger threat than under-diagnosis. The number of people diagnosed with mental illness in the UK doubled between 2002 and 2013. Dowrick believed millions were being treated for being simply sad or "down in the dumps". The problem began, he said, in the eighties when qualifying symptoms for depression were lowered.[5]

The term "pandemic", meanwhile, was ridiculously expanded to convert every limited and minor outbreak of disease into world-threatening proportions, often coinciding precisely with one of two things: annual budget reviews for the public health bureaucracies or mountains of unused vaccines in the warehouses of pharmaceutical firms.

The scare stories are as imaginative as they are endless. Initial estimates of deaths from Aids in Africa were subsequently found to be overstated by a factor of five. Avian Flu (H5N1), marketed as the killer of millions, carried away 379. The best runner was Swine Flu (H1N1). It killed 18 000 according to World Health Organisations' official stats, a fatality rate of 0.026%. Clearly not good enough for supercrisis.org: its research declared as many as 579 000 people had died, the toll largely achieved by enlisting as many fatalities from routine respiratory deaths as possible in the Swine Flu statistics. Stung by the paucity of its own ambitions, the WHO subsequently upped its numbers to 284 000 by an imaginative combination of guesswork, computer modelling and post facto diagnosis.

In the UK, where hysteria has become refined as the first response to scare, half a billion pounds worth of a vaccine against H1N1 was stockpiled for distribution through specially established call-centres for anybody who thought they had the symptoms. Tens of thousands were at risk, Britons were assured. In the end, of course, few died in the UK and it was not until 2014 that careful research by a team at Oxford University concluded that the vaccine at best reduced the symptoms by half a day and at worse had no more effect than an ordinary paracetemol pill.[6]

Another exemplar of managed panic was the Ebola haemorrhagic fever scare of late 2014. The disease has been endemic in West African societies since 1928 and probably from well before. Thousands had died from the disease, mourned but unremarked. In 1970, again in 1990 and then more extensively in 2014, there was an uptick in fatalities.

By end 2014, according to the World Health Organisation, there had been a total of slightly over 6 000 recorded fatalities from the disease. The major African killers of aids, malaria, typhoid and meningitis carry off over 1 800 000 people a year on the continent with hardly a raised eyebrow. Yet Ebola, accounting for less than 0.2% of this annual total in its *entire recorded life*, drove supercrisis.org and its supporting media into what can only be described as a paroxysm of scaremongering.

This panic became even more astonishing when one considers that the disease is transmitted by human-to-human contact and thus entirely containable with reasonable and appropriate measures in developed world countries, as difficult as they may be to apply in countries where cultural and other influences mitigate against rational control policies.

Behind the scare, lay supercrisis.org and its employees trying to earn a living in developed world economies where real jobs have largely been destroyed by the Egalitarian Fantasy. Scarcely had the crisis resolved, than the affected nations were campaigning for a "Marshall Plan" for their economies to recover from a disease that had been around for at least a century and most certainly longer.

The diagnosis of the pre-condition of diabetes, meanwhile, became so premature in the UK that respectable researchers at King's College, London, were compelled in 2014 to warn that huge numbers of people were being needlessly scared. Clearly, these researchers were not on the programme: they failed to grasp that scare *was* the point. Other research showed that the sacrosanct Body Mass Index numbers used by health authorities in the UK to diagnose conditions of overweight or obesity were too restrictive, undiscriminating and inappropriate. Indeed, credible research showed that humans in fact benefited from being a little overweight so as to have reserves when combating infections and longevity was improved in older people by having a few extra kilograms.[7]

The anti-tobacco lobbies provided a classic example of the resilience and versatility of the franchise. The lobby moved from commendable campaigns of educating people against the health risks of tobacco to becoming a fully fledged, multi-national operation determining legislation, enforcing restrictive measures, mounting economic campaigns against tobacco companies and stigmatizing smokers.

With the advent of electronic cigarettes and the possibility that millions of smokers might switch, anti-tobacco lobbies scented crisis for its multi-billion dollar franchise. Like a seal to water, they changed the tack of their approach to take on e-cigarettes on the basis that they did not end nicotine addiction, despite the fact that the device demonstrably reduced lung degradation and ended secondary inhalation --- something very important to families with young children.

The real tragedy in all of this effort by supercrisis. org, of course, was that desperately needed medical research in a huge range of illnesses became side lined as the researchers switched their attention to the celebrity diseases that would bring the big grants. The Aids epidemic of the late 20th Century was a perfect example. If even a fraction of the money spent on that project, worthwhile as it was, had been deployed, say, to finding a cure for Ebola, there would be no scare today. But then that would be naïve. Supercrisis.org would have simply found another one.

This entire fantasy crisis in health, however, camouflaged a real crisis --- one created directly by the Egalitarian Fantasy. The diminishing efficacy of antibiotics in treating a whole range of illnesses, some dread, had by the early part of the 21st century become identified as a patent and present danger by a range of credible research. The over-prescription of such drugs through decades had mutated a number of viruses and made them resistant to treatment by traditional antibiotics. This dangerously reduced the ability of the human organism to counter infection. The US Center for Disease and Control reported in 2013 that approximately two million Americans may well have been infected with anti-biotic resistant bacteria.

How had this happened? Two ways: the Egalitarian Fantasy had created open-ended and free national health systems which had been massively abused by developed world publics. A smorgasbord of freely available and endlessly prescribed drugs had critically lowered the resistance of the general public and, more specifically, that part of the public most prone to over-use the system and also the ones most likely to have the least healthy lifestyles---the lower socio economic groups.

But, secondly, the fear and guilt products of the health franchise of supercrisis.org had created a universal obsession by the public, particularly parents, to avoid "germs". Everything had to be sanitized, not least babies who were washed so clean with antiseptic soap that they fairly gleamed. Unable to build immunities to infections through excessive sanitization and faced with lower immunities to mutant viruses, the people of the developed world stood dangerously exposed to a new wave of pandemic infection --- real ones and not fantasy ones.

But here is the tragedy: by now the credibility of medical research had been so diminished through countless scare stories-- by a million shouts of wolf --that nobody believed it, a problem that was to afflict another of super-crisis.org's most profitable franchises, climate change, as we shall see later.

THE JUSTICE FRANCHISE

The judicial and quasi-judicial institutions also contributed mightily to this growth of fantasy functions and jobs and in so doing grievously undermined the core principles of proportionality, natural justice and due process. Ironically, the roots lie in the immediate aftermath of World War ll, a struggle waged ostensibly to assert the sanctity of the rule of law. Horrified by Nazi infamy, the Western elites decided that its perpetrators could not be prosecuted merely in terms of existing statute or criminal law but had to be prosecuted under a whole new category of war crimes and crimes against humanity.

It was not sufficient to charge the Nazi leadership with multiple murders, theft, damage to property, rape, arson, kidnap or assault in terms of the standard criminal provisions which existed in every legal jurisdiction in the world and would have resulted in the same justified conclusion --- death. They had to be charged in special courts, under special rules, by special prosecutors and before special judges. These rules and procedures, as we now know, departed from accepted jurisprudential practice, and to all intents and purposes made it impossible for the accused to escape conviction. It would have been more honest to follow Stalin's advice and have simply shot the top Nazis.

As brilliantly argued by Senior Counsel R T Paget in the trial of General Erich von Manstein in 1949, these were not criminal cases --- as they richly deserved to be --- but political ones. Instead of the Nazi elites being treated like the vile but common criminals they were, they became elevated to the status of political prisoners in danger of being made political martyrs by the extreme right.[1]

Tragically, the practice became embedded as the Egalitarian Fantasy gained traction. It was not the first total war exigency to be appropriated by The Egalitarian Franchises and repurposed so as to enable them to seize arbitrary powers and to enforce ideological outcomes. Suddenly whole swathes of actions which could be dealt with by existing law were elevated to crimes of such enormity that they demanded special designation --- hate crimes, sexual abuse, domestic violence, gender discrimination, human rights abuse, racial insult, "slavery" and so on. Inevitably, those most ideologically committed to combating these maladies came to dominate the institutions, create the precedents and write the law. They became in essence Courts of Inquisition, political and dogmatic organs dominated by those whose agenda was being served, all of it underpinned by Groupthink.

Its logical and terrifying end-point, of course, was the establishment in 2014 of self-appointed and semi-judicial tribunals sanctified by university authorities in the US and the UK, the last bunkers of the Egalitarian Fantasy, to try alleged sexual misdemeanours by students by Kangaroo rules. The rights of defendants were assailed. Common law was demeaned. Just law was the ultimate victim.

The most pernicious of these categories of "special law" was the evolution of so-called Hate Law, defined as crimes involving antagonistic actions towards a person because of their race, ethnicity, gender, religion, gender orientation, disability, looks or just about anything else that could be lumped into the category to create more potential victims. Such "Hate" could be expressed in any number of ways from murder right down to merely an askance look or asking the wrong question --- a UK woman was prosecuted in terms of Hate Speech law for asking a group of fellow-travellers on an underground train from whence they came. Her tone was deemed insulting and may well have been. But criminal?

Despite the fact that there was no conceivable aggressive act that one person could commit against another that was not already covered by provisions of existent criminal law, tens of thousands of people a year throughout the developed world were prosecuted under the catch-all provisions of the "Hate" laws. Why? Simple: prosecuting one person for being criminally insulting or aggressive to another does not make a political point. It does not serve The Egalitarian Fantasy. Prosecuting people in terms of Hate legislation does. It sends an unambiguous and intimidating message: when you are hostile or merely critical towards a person who is genetically and biologically different from the group into which you were born, you are entering into a new zone of political crime. Irrespective of whether the dispute has anything to do with race or ethnicity, you are still challenging the fundaments of The Egalitarian Fantasy. Beware.

The most insidious element in the armoury of Hate Law is Hate Speech. It is arguably the most powerful instrument for the suppression of freedom of speech in modern Western history. It is the main battle tank of The Egalitarian Fantasy in repressing dissent and penalising dissenters from the orthodoxy. Ironically, the very people who criticise Russia or China or Muslims for the repression of freedom of expression are most often the ones zealously supportive of suppressing freedom of speech in their own countries through the iniquitous provisions of Hate Law.

Thus British Prime Minister David Cameron could say in an interview with *Face the Nation* in January 2015 after the infamous massacre of the Charlie Hebdo cartoonists in Paris that: "I think in a free society, there is a right to cause offense about somebody's religion." But clearly not a right to refuse to undertake an abortion or officiate at a homosexual marriage on the grounds of religious conscience: that can get one banged up. Like Cameron, these liberal defenders of freedom of speech are sublimely unaware of their own inconsistency and hypocrisy.

Sadly, it all had its desired consequence. Discussion about ethnic or racial differences was chilled. Legitimate points of concern about the way individuals or groups behaved in a society was repressed. Open debate about the complexities of inter-racial or inter-group engagement was denied. Across the developed world, the indigenous populations were driven into a bitter, sullen and furtive silence about issues which materially affected their lives. Critical issues such as the growth of Islamic militancy and exceptionalism in Western society, the overwhelming of public services by mass immigration, unacceptable behaviour by groups from specific ethnic backgrounds, abuse of Western tolerance by new-comers to advance philosophies and actions that were the antithesis of core Western values, all of this was swept under the suffocating carpet of political correctness and outright coercion. Called upon to embrace "diversity", they were paradoxically threatened with prosecution if they discussed difference.

Hate Law's dread legacy was to found in the debates in Europe and the UK in late 2014 and early 2015 about how to combat Islamic extremists. In the wake of the atrocious and violent attacks by extremists on their critics and on Jews in general, Western governments pledged to crack down on "Hate Speech" on social media and elsewhere so as to prevent the incitement to violence.

But here the rub: Hate Speech had been made to refer as much to a person who unintentionally uses a few ill-thought words about a person's origins as to a person inciting others to cut off people's heads because of their religious affiliations. Once there would have been no problems: the former was crimen injuria and the latter incitement to violence. Statute law dealt with both adequately, appropriately and in context.

But Hate Law and its vicious half-brother, Hate Speech, had blurred the lines. No wonder public suspicion rose when politicians talked about tightening up Hate Speech laws. Who was the target of the new laws? Vile mass murderers ...... or the woman on the underground who asked fellow passengers from whence they came?

Flowing from that, inevitably, was the degradation of the credibility of Western political and legal institutions and the growth of extremist politics, something that will be discussed later in this essay.

THE VICTIM FRANCHISE

And under such conditions, of course, swathes of new jobs were created in the victim franchise of supercrisis. org. An entirely new phenomenon swept onto the stage: the professional victim. Whole classes of people defining themselves in racial, national, ethnic, religious and gender terms thrust themselves forward as victims to be recompensed for historic injustice.

In group terms it was a great gift to those who despite everything, had still failed to create successful and stable nations or productive communities. In individual terms, it was a particular grant to those who wished to force the rest of society to pay attention to some indignity, real or imagined, in their distant past.[1] For some, one must believe a tiny minority, it was merely a chance to make a quick buck or steal their 15 minutes of fame.

The tragedy, the limitless tragedy, was that the real victims of brutal mistreatment or sustained injustice, became swamped by the noise created by the armies of newly enrolled victims. Worse, in some cases they were swept away because their cases were deemed not noteworthy, not *political* enough.

Harold Bloom, an English Literature Professor and prolific, author pithily observed in his 1994 book, *The Western Canon:* "The final injustice of historical injustice is that it does not necessarily endow its victim with anything except a sense of their victimization."[2]

The skill of the Victim Franchise in maintaining a solid flow of victim fodder is best captured by a short biography of the evolution of "Hate" crimes in the UK. The country has long had legislation to combat race hatred and has meticulously tracked its incidence.

In 2008/9 there were 56 387 reported cases. The next year there were 55 056. Then 51 585 in 09/10; 47 678 in 10/11 and 35 816 in 2012/13. This amounted to a 36% decline in four years. If one thought this was an occasion for celebrating the advance of tolerant and cohesive societies, it was not. Supercrisis.org was horrified: they realised the race franchise had reached sell-by date.

The response was new legislation to define new crimes and to create a new institution: the Commission for Racial Equality gave way to the Commission for Equality and Human Rights. Hate crimes now included any expression of hostility towards anybody on the basis of disability, religion, race, gender-identity or sexual orientation. That, thought supercrisis.org, should do it.

But the 2011/12 official report under the new definitions reflected only 43 748 crimes --- less than had been recorded for race hate crimes alone under the previous designation. The next year showed a further decline to 42 236. Time for a hit-back, which duly came in the form of a 2013 report by the UK Departments of Justice and Home Affairs which entailed a changed reporting format.

Hate crimes are identified by the police reported crime register: in other words crimes real people thought worthwhile reporting to real police officers. Supplementing this was now a Crime Survey for England and Wales which sought to assess crime as experienced by the community, reported or not. Surveys, as we know, are wondrously malleable things and when whole sections of the society have been coached to feel victimised, the consequence is predictable.

Breitbart, an online news service reflecting conservative concerns in the UK, reports on the Green Party-led Brighton Council which issued a "Bullying and Prejudice Based Incident Report Form" to all schools in its jurisdiction, requiring teachers to classify all incidents according to "'ethnicity/race', 'appearance' (hair colour, body shape, clothing), 'disability/special needs' (including 'derogatory language' such as 'retard, spaz, geek, nerd'); 'gender identity' including 'someone who does not fit with gender norms or stereotypes'; 'home circumstances' such as 'class background' (calling another child 'chav, posh'); or 'sex' and 'sexual orientation',". Such, we can now fully grasp, is the rich diversity of "victimhood" sanctified, indeed encouraged, in modern UK.

With such an impeccably nurtured tradition of national victimology, the newly introduced crime survey unsurprisingly found *278 000* cases of self-identified hate crime --- seven times the official rate of reported incidents and a rate of overstatement even higher than the Health Franchise, the one stellar in its statistical extravagance. The following year, 2013/14, for the first time in six years, there was a slight uptick in registered hate crimes with the police. This may have been the consequence of several particularly provocative acts of violence by extremist Muslims in the UK. The less comforting notion is that once again, supercrisis.org had forced governmental bodies to align their numbers to serve the franchise.

A succession of cases was trailed through the British courts in 2013 and 2014, saying much about the obsessions of the prosecutorial service. But they were merely the latest in the 40 year long gestation of the phenomenon, and were not the only ones: failed ex-soldiers, alcoholics, drug addicts, partners in unsatisfactory relationships, failures in the work place, disabled people not willing to make the most of their disadvantage, the ailing of all classes, they all flocked to the calling of victimhood which by the early 21st Century had become the fastest growing occupational category in Anglo-Saxon economies.

A classic example of the expansion of the victim classes by law was the successive changes to the measures affecting domestic violence in the UK. Whereas once it was limited to physical assault, a common law offence, or failure to provide financial support, a civil and criminal offence, it was expanded to include things like psychological and emotional abuse and then to something called "dominating or controlling behaviour".

Yet underlying this continuous expansion of the definitions of the law, lay an astonishing fact. The 2014 Crime Survey of England and Wales --- a source noted more for its over than under statement of reality --- revealed that the incidence of domestic violence had been falling dramatically since 1993, by 75% in all, and was the lowest on record. Sexual assault was down 27%.

A visiting Martian would never have guessed that amidst all the 21st Century white noise surrounding the issue of domestic violence and the claims that it was rising that in fact the reverse was true: people in domestic arrangements were becoming more polite to each other, just as people of different races had been before the Egalitarian Fantasy's support of mass migration, foreign wars and general busy-bodying had heightened domestic tensions between groups. This thought was of course anathema to the ice maidens of the Victim Franchise and so they reacted typically: by a comprehensive redefinition and extension of the rules to a point where a senior UK Judge could observe that what once was merely bad manners had been reduced to punishable tort.

Not surprisingly, prosecutions soared and also, not surprisingly, nine out of ten of the accused admitted guilt rather than have to face trial. The activists in institutions like the UK's Crown Prosecutor's office saw this as a triumph and were entitled to a sense of satisfaction in ensuring that in real cases of abuse, justice had been visited. Underlying all of this and rarely mentioned, however, lay the uncomfortable suspicion that, whether by intent or not, an institutionalized, state-sanctioned form of extortion had been fashioned for unscrupulous women to use against males. And they did not even have to feel they were victims.

In perhaps the most chilling words ever uttered by a senior officer of Britain's modern legal system, a senior prosecutor told the BBC in an interview on April 11 2014, after yet another failed prosecution for a sex offence in which all the "victims" stated they did not consider themselves victims, that it was irrelevant if somebody thought they were a victim of a crime or not --- that was up to the prosecutor to decide. Even if they loved the alleged offender, or were cared for, they could still be victims without knowing it.

The Crown Prosecution Services also began issuing "guidance" instructing that complainants of rape were to be automatically granted the designation of "victim", rather than complainant, even if no decision by a court of law had been made. It argued the mere act of lodging a rape complaint with the police qualified the complainant for the status of victim.[3] Other guidance sought to instruct juries against "subconscious bias" in the treatment of rape. In some countries it might be considered jury coaching.

Just who was to be "victim" and whom "offender" in all this became grimly clear as increasingly large numbers of males --- in one case in the UK, a whole football team --- were peremptorily arrested on rape or sexual abuse charges on the say-so of a single woman. In many cases the accused were released without charge but not before the destruction of the reputation of the "offender". But this was not a victim the victim industry was prepared to embrace.

In a celebrated case in February 2015, a doctor, Dr Dhanuson Dharmasena, was acquitted of the charge of female genital mutilation on a newly-delivered young mother after the jury took no time in deciding the matter had nothing to do with FGM and everything to do with the appropriate clinical management of a pregnant woman. Once again, it appeared a trial launched by the Crown Prosecution Services in support of an ideological project, had failed.

so grave had this institutional bias by these legal systems in the UK become by 2014, that a senior family court judge, Judge David Tyzack, felt constrained to express his concern at the way the police and social services unquestioningly accepted the claims of the female partner without exercising their critical faculties.

"There is a very real danger in my judgment, of professionals treating the alleged victim's allegations as completely truthful and the alleged perpetrator as a sort of pariah."[4]

His comments followed a particularly gratuitous example of the distortion of due and fair process when a mentally unbalanced women fabricated a serious of charges against her ex-husband, all of which were demonstrably untrue but which the institutions had accepted without question.

And so the institutions deformed by The Egalitarian Fantasy, embarked on a relentless hunt for victims so as to justify the jobs of those self-appointed as the "victim's" defender. By 2014, 10% of cases handled by the Crown Prosecution Service related to "domestic violence" in its broadened terms --- this in a year when it was estimated 400 000 punishable criminal offences such as affray, assault, burglary, theft and carjacking had been dealt with "administratively" and never brought to court at all. And a year in which it was confirmed serious domestic violence had declined by 75% in 15 years.

Predictably, the number of "support groups" established to extend assistance to the soaring numbers of victims of "domestic abuse", each competing for state support, had become of a scale in the UK by 2014 that steps were underway to "regulate" the industry.

Indeed, so desperate became this Burke and Hare search for victims, that the Egalitarian Fantasy franchises in the UK were forced to reach back into the distant past to resurrect "victims" or, to be politically correct, "survivors", of alleged malfeasance by individuals, usually male, or institutions, mainly the security forces, from literally decades earlier.

How did this play out in financial and institutional terms? No better exemplar can be found than in the legal aid regime in the UK. In 2014 the Council of Europe reported that the UK had the most lawyers in the EU and paid the most in legal aid. The total bill to the taxpayer was £2bn. In France it was £290mn and in Germany £272mn. The average EU bill was £97mn. Cost per head in the UK was £26 while in the EU the average was £7.[5] Even if one accepts the argument that the Inquisitorial method of justice in European countries puts the burden of cost on the Judge rather than the lawyer, the differential in spend is still material.

Here again was the Egalitarian Fantasy at work. In order to create fantasy jobs, the UK legal system needed victims. It could not get enough real victims --- crime was declining, employment on the up and real poverty receding --- so it manufactured them. In the first instance it was done by expanding the definition of "crime", as in the case of domestic abuse or Hate Law, or by reaching back into the past, as in the case of so-called historic sex crimes. In the second instance the *criminals* were miraculously also converted into victims so that they too could provide employment for the middle-class counsellors, defenders, protagonists and promoters thronging the sally ports of supercrisis.org. Thus the provision of legal aid was massively expanded so that all may feed from this bounteous trough.

Again, this had nothing to do with meeting a need or creating fairness and justice. It was about creating jobs. The consequences were of course appalling and not just in financial terms. A litigious culture flourished, criminal acts became low risk, a sense of impunity abounded and at the end of it all, ordinary, decent people were called upon to pick up the tab.

THE ENVIRONMENT FRANCHISE

Undoubtedly the most successful franchise of supercrisis.org has been the environmental scare of the late 20th and early 21st centuries, a classic example of the inflation of genuine concerns about environmental issues in an industrialised world into either a rent-seeking opportunity or an ideological project of the Egalitarian Fantasists.

Again, it is important to make the usual disclaimers lest we be led down pointless cul de sacs. No serious person would dispute that major environmental challenges exist in the post-modern world, not least the need to limit dependence on finite fossil fuel reserves, reduce pollution, protect natural green spaces, prepare our countries to be resilient to adverse weather conditions if they occur and conserve energy usage. Many hugely useful local initiatives to achieve all of the above have been underway for years. For more than 70 years, to use a down-to-earth example, the Boy Scout movement ran paper and glass recycling schemes and anti litter campaigns.

The problem comes when a deeply unsettled science is promoted as the compelling reason why we should take actions which materially and dangerously undercut economic sustainability in the developed world and, by extension, the developing one. It becomes even less comprehensible when such actions are flagrantly in the financial or ideological interests of vested interests and so clearly injurious to so many others.

Let us again state the case. This Essay does not deny that the climate is changing and indeed marginally warming. Our planet is in a state of constant evolution and we have always moved between periods of climatic tranquillity to turbulence and back, from warming periods to cooling ones. What this Essay does observe is that the linkages between green house gas emissions, primarily CO_2, and climate change are still imperfectly understood; that the climate warming models produced by the experts have been routinely confounded for nearly two decades and that the role of anthropogenic climate change remains in serious dispute --- only four per cent of CO_2 emissions are down to humans and latest research indicates that the natural release of the gas from below the sea is of such a scale that it dwarfs any puny contribution made by humans.

Despite these huge qualifications to the whole scientific premise of climate change, challenges which in any rational business or well administered state would demand much more convincing evidence before critical investment or policy decisions, the developed world has precipitously embarked on far-reaching, perhaps irreversible, economic processes ostensibly on the basis of the need for "insurance". These decisions, this Essay argues, were not in fact based primarily on a belief in the climate change crisis at all but were an integral part of the fantasy job creation programme which itself was a direct result of the developed world's failed Egalitarian Fantasy.

Consider: a planet that is capable of sustaining average global temperature variations of above 10 degrees C daily was suddenly held to be in mortal danger because it had warmed 0.8 degrees Celsius in *140 years[1]*; years encompassing the industrial revolution, two World Wars, mass air travel and a huge growth in human population. By 2013 the planet had not materially warmed for 17 years and the actual global temperatures were tracking at the very bottom range of the doomsday composite projections of the Climate Warmists. Indeed, they were about to fall off the graph altogether.[2] Real planetary temperatures were by 2014 only a quarter of what the Warmists' composite models in 2007 had with relish predicted they would be by that year.

When the inconvenient truth emerged that no coherent link could be established between global temperatures and CO_2 levels in the atmosphere, the "science" discovered that the world *had* warmed to the extent of the projections. It was just that this warmth was trapped below the oceans but it would take us at least ten years to determine whether the hypothesis was correct.[3] It was not the only proposal. By 2014 there were 52 complete hypotheses by the Climate Change scientists to account for this embarrassing "pause" in warming. When all this sounded a little tendentious to the broad public, the science and its supportive media backed off trying to fit CO_2 up for global warming and instead accused it of causing "extreme" weather, with as little supporting scientific evidence.[4]

Hardly had this change of tack been agreed than one could hear the figurative clicking of a thousand word processors formulating new research grant applications to investigate every example of extreme weather phenomenon. Inevitably, the events were declared to be worst ever and more proof of the impact of hot house gases. Ignored was the fact that climate measurement techniques had vastly improved since earlier centuries thus making comparisons tendentious, density of human habitation had worsened vulnerability to extreme weather, built environments had exacerbated the impact of inclement weather and, not least, vast media and supercrisis.org industries had sprung up whose vested interest lay in exaggerating natural events.

These serious questions were swept aside by the United Nation's Intergovernmental Panel on Climate Change in its Fifth Assessment report of 2013. The "probability" that humans were damaging the environment, it claimed, had escalated from 90% to 95%.[5], thus displaying one of the unique skills of the environmental franchise of supercrisis.org, its capacity to align a whole range of diverse and hugely enriched vested interests under one sanctimonious Mother Theresa brand. It was this unity of purpose, coupled with the promise of "Saving the Planet", that enabled this franchise of supercrisis.org to surmount the fragility, indeed contradictions, of the underlying scientific argument.

Mustered under the franchise came investment brokers in Green Bonds, fresh from their richly destructive pickings in the US sub-prime market and collaterised debt obligations; dealers of the same ilk desperate to resurrect a discredited world carbon credit trade; manufacturers of renewable energy equipment which was marketed on risibly over-stated projections of their power generation capacities and job multipliers; mendicants from poor countries seeking yet another opportunity of ripping the ring from fatigued Western aid agencies and, finally, the liturgically anti-capitalist lobbies orphaned by the collapse of communism and looking for new ways to cripple Western economies. In the environmental issue the latter found a tool which succeeded beyond their wildest dreams; infinitely more efficacious than grinding, *passe* old communism.

Underpinning all of this were the justifying mythologies spun by the climate change scientists, an enclosed group of self-reinforcing advocates, endlessly washing each other's hands, peer reviewing each other's work, sharing the same research grants, collaborating on how best to present the evidence to advance the cause, consulting to the same environmental corporates, fronting the same media chat shows, and falling further and further into Groupthink. For them, the substantial body of scientists sceptical about the wildest claims of the environmentalist posed a poisonous threat whose views had to be repressed --- and for a considerable period were.

The consequences of all this fantasy work in the "Green Sector" were appalling.[6]

The economic competitiveness of the developed world plunged on the back of high energy costs thus driving unemployment (and thus more supercrisis.org interventions)[7], fuel poverty became a reality for many Western households (prompting more supercrisis.org work supporting the "vulnerable")[8], world food markets were distorted by biofuel industries leading to real hunger (and thus promising yet more supercrisis.org work)[9] and biomass enterprises drove up the cost of hard wood for low cost residential housing (and even more supercrisis.org busy-bodying to help the "homeless")[10].

An exemplar of what happens when public policy moves beyond fantasy to absurdity, in this case with Teutonic thoroughness, must be German energy policy. The cost of the green levies to fund renewable technologies had by 2014 raised consumer and industrial costs of energy to uncompetitive levels; indeed Germans were paying by 2013 €16bn in subsidies for €3bn worth of electricity and in late 2014 BASF, a chemical giant, was one of the first big corporates to admit it was moving productive capacity away from Germany because of high energy costs.

The high levels of subsidies to renewables, meanwhile, had lowered the wholesale price of energy so that conventional gas and coal fleets became uncompetitive. A quarter of this fleet was closed and the rest kept going by, yes, subsidies. As coal and gas prices plummeted in 2014, the cost of subsidies to renewables increased. The country's nuclear reactors, meanwhile, had been shut in deference to Green sensibilities. German reliance on Russian gas made it vulnerable during the Russo-Ukrainian crisis of 2014. To remedy this self-induced crisis, Germany began building lignite powered electricity stations with 30 year life spans, relying on vastly more polluting fuels. Coal consumption had risen 4.9% since the closure of the nuclear power stations; carbon emissions by 1.3% in 2013 alone.

No sane economic policy could underwrite such an Alice In Wonderland outcome. So why do it? It was certainly not because the eco-industrialists were concerned about green house gases. When cheap Chinese solar panels swamped western countries in 2014, the European manufacturers of panels stampeded to Brussels to demand higher import charges and thus higher costs for renewable energy. So much for saving the planet.

The clue was given by Manual Barroso, President of the EU Commission in 2012 when he hailed renewable energy as the most important job creator in Europe in decades. So there it was: fantasy jobs in a fantasy industry to pursue fantasy objectives --- thanks to the Egalitarian Fantasy.

But worst of all, entirely legitimate concerns about environmental issues were diminished, not enhanced by the alarmism of the eco-entrepreneurs and watermelon ideologues. Critical issues became swamped in the noise created by the clamorous supercrisis.org vested interests, to the point where huge numbers of otherwise sympathetic people simply switched off. Google, for example, saw an 84% plunge in searches for "Global Warming" between 2007 and 2014. The broad public had been driven to indifference, boredom or scepticism by the excesses.

AND YET MORE FRANCHISES

The "crisis" of lack of success of groups from the lower socio-economic levels was elevated by the simple expedient of pushing the definition of "success" ever upwards. An American sociologist once famously remarked that all a young person had to do to be successful was to stay in school, avoid teenage pregnancy and turn up for work on time. Such sensible and gettable criteria were of course ignored by the franchise. Success was measured not by a simple yardstick of employment, inter-personal stability, personal self-responsibility, self sufficiency or even personal happiness but had miraculously become the need to be a graduate --- a calculatedly absurd hurdle for people with epigenetically impaired working memories but a

great boon to the educational establishment and in particular "transformational teachers".[1]

The International Aid Franchise of supercrisis.org has
been so exhaustively analysed and commented upon that
it merits only passing mention in this Essay. Perhaps no
greater example of the absurdity of the Egalitarian Fantasy
can be found than the fact that the European Union countries have committed themselves to devoting 0.7% of
their GDP to foreign aid --- although one can be assured
that few honour it.

The point is that it is an arbitrary number. It is not derived by annual assessments of real need. It is not modified
as global circumstances change. It is not increased in cases
of demonstrable need or reduced in times of tranquillity.
Above all, it pays no attention to whether this aid is wisely
used or not. It is just a number, a statistic, and it serves
no greater purpose that assuaging the consciences of the
Egalitarian Fantasists.

There are three simple and immutable laws affecting fixed rate annuity income. As turn-over grows,
the annuity income increases; as annuity income increases, needs are manufactured to meet the income;
as needs are generated to meet the income, staff numbers are generated to meet the manufactured needs to
match the growing funding. That is precisely the trap

into which the developed world has fallen with such idiocy.

The laxity in which foreign aid has been both spent and targeted, approximately three trillion dollars in the last sixty years, is the subject of numerous books, the two foremost probably being William Eastley's *The White Man's Burden: Why The West's Efforts To Aid The Rest Have Done So Much Ill And So Little Good (2006),* and Dambiso Moyo's *Dead Aid: Why Aid Is Not Working And How There Is A Better Way For Africa. (2009).* Apart from the wordiness of titles, the books are similar in that they make essentially the same point: Western Aid, for all its good intentions, has served to support corrupt and authoritarian regimes, increase dependency in places like Africa and create a self-sustaining bureaucracy. Moyo, a Zambian economist, went further: critics in the Aid Franchise accused her of calling for the termination of aid within five years although she insisted this was a misinterpretation. Bill Gates, superbenefactor to supercrisis.org branded her work "evil".

There were also rich fields of human misery abroad to be harvested: war, famine, pestilence, all grist to supercrisis.org's mill. No greater example of the importance of the raw product of human misfortune could be found than in 2006 when the then isolationist Government of Myanmar refused to allow in aid workers after devastating floods. The paroxysm of rage from the NGO's went well beyond care for the unfortunates involved: it was an existential threat to supercrisis.org's business model.[2]

Profitable offshoots from this was of course international "Peace Keeping" or "Peace Making", endeavours which opened vast new employment opportunities for administrators, facilitators and humanitarian interventionists and secured, on the other hand, revenue streams for the deployed forces, many from poor countries. In short, it was just another transfer system whereby both wealthy and poor countries created new jobs.[3]

But by 2014, supercrisis.org was running out of steam amongst the broad public in western countries although, sadly, not amongst the political and academic classes. Its original *raisons d'etre* were flagging. Neither famine nor refugees could raise a jaded public interest: there was too little of the former and too many of the latter. The developing world had been so thoroughly turned on its head by reckless Western interventions that the instinct of most Western publics was to withdraw, keep their heads below the parapet and most certainly not engage militarily.

The racism franchise was also flagging. Across the Western world the reported incidents of race hate were falling, despite every attempt to broaden its scope and the adroit efforts by the franchise to confuse opposition to Muslim extremism with racism so as to sustain the subversion of core western values and grow the victim pool. Although the feminism franchise was still barrelling along thanks to special interest groups and the political elites' pursuit of the women's vote, it too was puffing. The overwhelming weight of research showed that support for extremist feminism, most specifically amongst women, was fast fading as the absurd consequences became daily more apparent, as we will discuss later in this essay. The Western elites were always way, way behind shifting public opinion so it was just a matter of time.

But where to now? Although religious tensions were rising in the wake of the crisis caused by Western interventions in the Middle East notably from the 2003-Iraq war-onward, this was a difficult one for supercrisis.org to engage. It was too political, too ambiguous and too risky. There was no upside. Besides, supercrisis.org did not *do* God or its institutions, apart from when bare breasted tatterdemalion feminists occasionally desecrated the sanctity of Christian places of worship --- never Mosques or Synagogues --- to make some obtuse ideological point.

Supercrisis.org had to find a new mission. It did in 2014: slavery. Something that had been effectively dealt with in the early 19th century, apart from residual and economic remnants in Arabic countries, had been resurrected as a new "crisis". It was suddenly discovered that 30 million people on the planet lived in "slavery".[+] The opportunities for the misery industries were enormous, the supply of victims limitless, and so began the usual tiresome and destructive processes.

Across the globe slavery "crisis" groups driven by middle-class sentiment and the prospects of yet more rent taking began to gather and secure political and financial support. The media leapt at the opportunity. Western politicians, keen to justify their salaries, formulated laws to raise "slavery" to another special instance of criminality higher than normal legal process, despite the fact that a plethora of existing laws relating to kidnapping, intimidation, immigration violations, breach of health and employment conditions and so on amply covered the issue. Indeed, forced labour is outlawed in virtually every jurisdiction in the world except for some countries with archaic indenture practices. But this had nothing to do with law; everything to do with creating another job multiplier for the Western middle classes. Thus grew the laws, institutions, personnel and mythology to justify another surge of fantasy employment creation; another wave of dreary and impenetrable terminology.

MOPPING UP THE REST

In its unswerving pursuit of fantasy job creation, the post modern state also massively expanded a theme that

had been developing in Stage Two: qualification inflation in the interests of fantasy job creation. In the place
of simple apprenticeships as *entrée* to medium-skilled
jobs came elaborate and lengthy periods of tutelage
followed by preliminary qualification topped by final
qualification.

Years and years were spent by young people to become
entry level nurses or rookie policemen when in the past it
had been accomplished by six month or one year training
programmes followed by on-the-job learning. The objective was not to make people better qualified at their work
--- the universal decline in public perceptions of the quality of public service delivery gives the lie to this --- but
to *make work*. The process, in some instances morphing
workers into a state of semi-permanent tutelage, did nothing to improve national competence or competitiveness.
But it certainly made the unemployment numbers look
better and it hugely boosted the population of fantasy jobbers in the educational establishments.[1]

The over-elaboration in the training of the most basic
of occupational functions, meanwhile, meant indigenous
people were just not available or interested in doing menial functions. The classic example was in the NHS where
simple things like patient hygiene and procedural issues
like inserting catheters was outsourced to foreign-trained
health workers, most from poorer countries.

Everybody had a slice of the action. The media were willing promoters of this fantasy job creation programme and in particular the innovative products of supercrisis. org – indeed, institutions like the British Broadcasting Corporation with its 8 000 journalists alone were exemplars of the programme. Human Resource practitioners and labour consultants reaped huge profits. Consultants rejoiced. The legal profession waxed lyrical and rich in the process. The public injury litigation industry reached unparalleled levels of profitability as it threw itself behind the "Health and Safety" regimes promoted by the brigades of fantasy jobbers.

Astonishingly, the shrillness of supercrisis.org's lamentations seemed to rise in inverse ratio to the success of its ostensible objectives. In the UK, for example, road deaths declined by a factor of 3.5 between 1980 and 2010. Whereas in 1948, 52% of adults smoked, by 2010 it was 20%. Habitual drinking plunged from 72% of adults in 2005 to 58% in 2012.[2] But nowhere were these positive changes in people's lifestyles acknowledged. The reverse: this very success appeared to be regarded by supercrisis. org as some sort of provocation. Its hysteria, intrusiveness and clamour for attention, draconian solutions and money simply increased. Born to war, it searched endlessly for new campaigns.

In the process of course, costs of services rose to cover insurance claims, age-old public festivals, customs and traditions were subverted and children discouraged from enjoying normal, exuberant childhoods. The greyness of caution, fear, uniformity and timidity fell like a curtain across the developed world; it fell like an iron curtain. It was another pernicious form of social control by increasingly authoritarian governments.[3]

But even after all of that --- the nonsense jobs created in the state and through supercrisis.org --- there were still those sitting jobless. These ones the State simply paid to stay at home and imported legions of under-educated foreigners to do the work those staying at home could and should have done. The Egalitarian Fantasy naturally demanded that these newcomers should also enjoy nearly all the benefits of indigenous people.[4]

When even a massive expansion of the welfare support system proved insufficient to deal with the new legions of can't works and will not works, some governments, like the British socialists and successive US administrations, deemed perfectly healthy men and women to be disabled to get them off the unemployment lists. The number of people on disability allowances in the UK increased ten-fold between 1969 and 2013 --- and this at a time of booming investment in health care and an improved knowledge of nutrition.[5] And then the state employed "carers" to look after these otherwise healthy people. The next step, obviously, was the establishment of carer support groups to care for the carers. And then carers of the carers who cared. And so absurdly on.

IN THE CRAZY ZONE

The preceding sections have sought to trace by random example the causal links between The Egalitarian Fantasy and the destruction of western competitiveness. Inequality in the capacity of individuals and groups to rise to opportunity led to an unsustainable growth in the social cost of labour in the interests of "equality". This caused falling labour productivity in the advanced economies, something to be discussed in detail later, and an exodus of low to middle level jobs to developing economies. This drop in employment led in turn to the creation of fantasy jobs and the emergence of a huge advocacy sector, labelled above, as the reader will have noticed by now, supercrisis.org, all committed in some form or other to promoting the Egalitarian Fantasy.

This sector had two effects. First, it had a deforming and anti-competitive impact on the advanced economies, leading to further job losses and more fantasy job creation. Second, it created a pervasive sense of fear, insecurity and despair in western societies. No crisis ever seemed to be resolved. Nothing that was done led to improvement.

Whatever solutions were proposed became drowned by contestation, debate, acrimony, all of it waged by self-proclaimed "experts" with whom the broad public had not the slightest identification. There was no apparent political leadership to take charge: they were all evidently intimidated into blandness, suffused with cliché, riddled with contradiction. The vicious cycle was complete.

By the Noughties the developed world had entered the Crazy Zone. Except for a few pockets of manufacturing excellence, primarily in Northern Europe and the United States, the economies of the developed world were uncomfortably dependent on a large public sector, a precariously balanced financial services sector (itself battened onto an insanely booming property sector) and, lastly, consumer spending generated by wealth transfers to armies of people either retired, on welfare entitlements or doing fantasy work in the governmental or neo-governmental sectors.

Composite Central Intelligence Agency and International Monetary Fund statistics showed that by 2014, the European Union was accounting for 53% of all global social welfare spend yet producing 18% of world GDP. The United States accounted for 31% of welfare expense yet also provided only 18% of global GDP. China, accounting for 15% of world GDP, claimed a mere four per cent of world welfare investment. It does not take a rocket scientist to work out that the advanced economies were seriously unbalanced in terms of social welfare spending relative to their GDP.

Needless to say, none of this created general value or wealth; indeed it detracted from it. The gap between the capacity to create wealth and the costs of supporting the Egalitarian Fantasy in all its multi-faceted derivatives became huge. The governments of the developed world could bridge it only one way. They took on vast, unimaginable, crippling levels of debt.

In 1913, the level of government debt by the 13 most advanced industrial nations was 12% of GDP. By 1990, it was 43%. If one hoped the crisis of 2007/08 would lead to a major push-back against debt, it did not happen. By 2013, average EU government debt was still 106.9% of GDP, according to OECD numbers. In the UK alone, public debt rose from 36% of GDP in 2007 to 61% in 2011. Total debt, public and private, stood at 275% of GDP by 2014, having increased by 20% since the crisis of 2008.

A European Central Bank Working Paper[1] argued that any debt ratio above 90% of GDP must inevitably lead to long term damaging effects. This was a theme developed by Harvard economists Carmen Reinhart and Kenneth Rogoff who argued that countries with debt ratios above 90% suffered a two per cent hit on growth compared with those with ratios below 30%. The findings led to hysterical denunciations by the advocates of the Debt Franchise who perfectly understood that to keep the Egalitarian Fantasy alive, developed world countries would have to maintain ruinous public and private debt levels. But how?

And so to the Fifth Stage on the road to irrelevance, the final one. This was the Debt for Wealth project.

Defeated now on every front in their hopes of advancing the interests of the majority of the poor, two leftist American Presidents rolled the last dice. If poor people could not all be advanced through education, or direct cash transfers, or inflated earnings or titles, or by attacking the elites or by creating fantasy jobs, or through the welfare state, or by affirmative action, or by being declared physically or mentally incapable or by being put into permanent tutelage, or by being declared "slaves" or "victims", if none of this worked, then at least they could be made to *feel* less poor by giving them credit. And so we come to the Community Reinvestment Act, enacted by President Carter and implemented by President Clinton, that forced US banks against their will to lend money to the African-American and Hispanic minorities, despite a risk profile 39% worse than other communities in the US.[2]

In the early days of its roll-out, the CRA's protagonists focused on the loan flows into the target communities. Enhanced powers of intimidation were passed to community groups to harass those institutions trying to maintain nominal risk control measures. It had its effect: all restraint was abandoned by the financial institutions as they competed for share of the loan market. In its latter days, even community groups warned about the risks being incurred by unsecured loans to "fragile" communities.

On its own, this would have been easily managed by an economy the size of the United States', as indeed it had managed such crises on many occasions before, most notably the savings and loans scheme of the 1980s where banksters were jailed in their dozens. But there were other factors at stake which led to the proverbial Perfect Storm in 2008.

Cheap Chinese money flooded into the US housing market via wholesale financing.[3] And then the usual suspects, those who through centuries of Western history have always preyed on the weak and gullible, devised a system of collateralising the debt, cutting and dicing it and reselling it like bags of mixed-grade potatoes in terms of formulae nobody could understand and whereby nobody knew who owed what to whom.[4] Unimaginable amounts of debt remained tethered to small and diminishing real assets. And then the borrowers defaulted, just as the banks had warned they would, and the bankers woke up to discover they had not the slightest idea of the worth of the assets they held.

Underlying this whole process was an equally impla-cable and menacing manipulative process at work --- the maintenance of artificially low levels of interest by the de-veloped world's central banks. The left-wing revisionist history of the period insists this was done solely to enrich the elites, that it was the worst face of capitalism possible. Well, no. The real reason for these low rates was not pri-marily to feed the rich, but to sustain the poor and to fund the voracious monster that was the Egalitarian Fantasy. It worked two ways: low interest rates encouraged invest-ment (good) and promoted excessively high personal debt (bad). Working together, they pushed up the price of as-sets, particularly relative to the poor, to astonishing levels.

The easy flow of credit to US homeowners allowed them to remortgage their homes multiple times on the back of crazily rising property prices. Tragically but predictably, little of this windfall was reinvested into productive assets. It was monetised and instantly consumed. The American Enterprise Institute reported in 2012 that by 2008, the Federal Housing Administration held 4.5m sub prime loans and the Federal-sponsored housing agencies, Freddie Mae and Freddie Mac, held 10 million. Private banks were on the hook for 2.7 million sub prime loans. Then the crash. House prices went into free-fall and without the reserves to withstand the onslaught, homeowners went into epic default. Within a year, 45% of household wealth of those under 40 years of age in the US had been wiped out.

Predictably, there was a wholesale heading-for-the hills at this point as everybody disclaimed responsibility. Numerous inquiries in the United States sought to emphasise that bad debts occurred as much in prime markets as sub-prime. It was a typical case of post-crisis Egalitarian Fantasy dissimulation. The CRA had precipitated the collapse of sound lending practice which had infected the whole system: by the end of this catastrophe the CRA had succeeded in reducing good and bad debt to one unholy mess.

The third crucial link in sustainable economies, the one between the *price* and the *value* of assets had been ruptured. The third light on the console lit up. It was blood red. The Egalitarian Fantasy had turned terminal.

The conservative and prudent fundamentals which had by and large characterized Western banking institutions quite simply buckled under the impact of this ill-informed and catastrophic political intervention in lending policies. The culture of swash-buckling and quick-rich investment banking swamped that of the cautious and long-term retail banking sector --- a point made by Sir Roy Killop, then Chairman of the Royal Bank of Scotland, in evidence before the UK House of Commons inquiry into the collapse of major banks in late 2008. The consequences were entirely predictable: fraudulent dealings in financial instruments, Ponzi scams of epic proportions, Libor rates fixing, manipulation of other rates and indexes, credit insurance frauds and a pervasive sense of trickery, sleaze and dishonesty.

The impact of all this on developed world societies went well beyond mere financial loss. It struck at the very heart of the most important element making for successful modern states --- interpersonal trust and trust in institutions. In April 2008, 58% of Americans said they had trust in their fellow countrymen. Only 38% of South Americans and Africans felt the same way about their fellow countrymen.[5]. By 2012, after the financial collapse, American public trust in institutions had collapsed to 40%. In short, public trust had fallen to the level of the developing world, had been degraded to its lowest levels ever ---- thanks to the myth that all individuals were the same and would respond in the same way to opportunity, one of the critical building blocks of the Egalitarian Fantasy.[6]

THE FINANCIAL COST IN SNAPSHOT

The consequence for the developed world of nearly six decades of the Egalitarian Fantasy is profound. The most important result has been the shift from investment in *equity* --- the investment in productive capacity --- to *debt*. The former builds roads and businesses and airports and bridges and factories and brings technical advance. The latter, overwhelmingly, was used by the developed world to subsidise the Egalitarian Fantasy, to pay for welfare systems, generous pension schemes, public servants, brigades of people in supercrisis.org and their costly and destructive projects.

A few snapshot numbers capture the scale of the hole the Egalitarian Fantasy had dug for the developed world by 2013.

Total world debt, private and public, was $270tr by 2012. Total equity capital was $65tr. In short, debt was three times the size of equity markets or, put another way, for every $1 of assets there existed $3 of debt.[1] In 1960, of every one dollar raised in debt, 59 cents pumped straight back into supporting economic growth. By 2012 it was 18 cents.[2] The rest was squandered on welfare, payment of debt interest and speculation.

The scale of the debt was frightening. In the UK, now the world's fifth largest economy, the debt of companies rose from 45% of GDP to more than 90%. Productive assets, once largely paid for in cash, became in increasingly financed by debt. UK's bank assets had grown from 70% of national income in 1970 to more than 450% in 2014. Thanks to an unprecedented Quantitive Easing, or Weimar-style erosion of currency value, the US Federal

Reserve's assets had grown from less than one trillion dollars to more than four trillion. Half hearted efforts at controlling debt, capitalizing banks and easing monetary supply in the wake of the 2008 financial crisis had virtually no impact. Six years after the crisis, debt in the developed world had risen another 20% and was touching 275% of GDP, according to OECD statistics.

The trigger point for this mass creation of debt in the Anglo Saxon countries was the late 1980's and early 90's. Why? Because this is when the building Egalitarian Fantasy conceived by the immediate post-war generation finally came to fruition; the point at which the monthly invoices had started rolling. This debt, it needs to be endlessly repeated, was not primarily raised to make rich people richer --- they were already beyond the point where they needed credit and indeed, as savers they were penalized by lower rates --- but to subsidise poorer people in the hope that *they* could become richer. Some did become richer, those with the innate ability to rise to the opportunity. Most did not.

By 2013, the US's dollar-denominated debt stood at a heart-stopping $1.7tr. If one took the US's 2012 accounts as those of an ordinary household it would read thus: Income: $ 21 700; Expenditure: $ 38 200; Existing Debt: $142 710; New 2012 Debt: $16 500. In response to this horrific situation, President Obama proposed his solution in 2012: a $38.50 cut in expenses. Not surprisingly, his opponents opted instead for a pre-agreed mandatory cut in public expenditure.

How this debt arose is easy to answer. In 1960, for every pensioner in the UK there were 18 working people. By 2012 there were five.[3] By 2013, pensioners in the UK were coming on stream at the rate of quarter a million a year. On average they would live about 19 years. Only seven of these years were funded. The average personal savings by a UK pensioner in 2012 was $10 500.[4] Why should they have bothered to save? The Egalitarian Fantasy had told them they would enjoy cradle to the grave security.

In 1960, for every American on disability allowance, there were 134 workers. By 2012 there were 18.[5] In the UK, the abuse of the system of medical disability allowances had by 2013 reached material proportions: the Government's own statistics indicated that only one in eight disability grant recipients could be deemed to be incapable of doing any work and approximately one third of recipients had no right to claim disabilities even under then eligibility rules.[6]

In the UK, model of much that occurred later in European states and foreshadowing what was to happen in the US under its redistributive President Barack Obama, the share of welfare spending as a proportion of GNP was one per cent in the 1940's. By the time the socialists exited power in the UK in 2010, it was eight per cent. European Union states, hastening to follow, were by 2012 consuming 53% of the world's *total* welfare spend although only producing 18% of the world's GDP.[7]

If the expense side of the ledger was grave, the income side was worse.

The world's richest economies had for 50 years seen a trended slow decline in the real growth rate of GDP per person, correlating almost exactly with the onset of the Egalitarian Fantasy.[8] The median rate had fallen from four per cent per year in the 1960's to just 0.02% after 2008 and then flat lining in real terms. The contribution of developed world households to their own maintenance had accordingly plummeted.

In 1977, 40% of UK households took out more from the economy in benefits than it put back in taxes. By 2012 it was 53%, although it moderated slightly to 52% by 2014.[9] In 2012 only one region in the UK out of seven, the south east, contributed more to national wealth than it consumed.[10] In the twelve years since 2000, the native born population of the UK alone made a negative contribution to the economy of $886 bn as the country ran deficits in its scramble to fund the Egalitarian Fantasy[11] By 2012 the number of households making no contribution to Federal taxes in the US was 47%.[12] The redistributive Presidency of Obama hastened the process.

The reason for this collapse of household viability is obvious. In 2012 the average working week in the UK was 32 hours. If one averages it out to include the five million economically active not working but who could, it was 26 hours: half the working week of the average British person a generation earlier.[13] Worse, research in 2013 in the UK indicated that the average worker was only productive 3.5 hours in a normal working day, the rest being taken up with socializing and social media.[14] Statistics released by the UK Department of Work and Pensions in 2014 showed that in any one year up to 900 000 British workers were off for longer than four weeks with illness --- many of them related to "depression".[15]

Some research indicated the average school goer in the US spent half as much time on homework, meaning formal assignments, in 2012 as did the previous generation.[16] The lost time was swallowed up by social media and internet, themselves pursuits which were billed as "democratizing" forces but in fact, research has indicated, has atomised sequential thought patterns in lower intelligence young people, isolated them, made them socially inept and envious, caused them to develop addiction patterns similar to chronic gamblers and has created platforms for unparalleled levels of peer intimidation and bullying. The political impacts are dealt with later.[17]

Not surprisingly, developed world capacity to generate growth had been shot to hell, By 2013 it was saddled with burdensome costs, not just for supporting its welfare systems but for servicing its significant debts. Conversely its capacity to generate wealth was gravely reduced.

The response to this bubble of debt by the developed world merely exacerbated the problem. Both the US and British central banks began what was euphemistically called Quantitative Easing which, rudely translated, meant the printing of billions of units of money so that Governments could buy back their debts. This virtual money --- funny money if you wish --- seeped not into productive purposes but the stock markets which boomed. All of this, remember, on falling productivity and stagnant wage levels. In short, the rich became richer and the poor poorer.

And thus the toxic link between the investment in an unproductive and ideological Egalitarian Fantasy had led directly to massive debt creation and from that to money printing and from thence to another ratchet in the gap between the rich and the poorer.

Prior to this madness, four pillars had throughout five centuries upheld Western wealth formation: dominance in the technology of manufacturing process; control of intellectual property; preferential access to raw materials and markets though the colonies and dominance in the financial markets. After 60 years of the Egalitarian Fantasy, the first three pillars had been largely ceded to other countries and the fourth was crumbling.

THE END OF INNOVATION?

The developed world's last hope, the rabbit which through time has always been pulled from the hat, technological step-change to create new waves of wealth, now has limited influence. This is a controversial but defensible proposition. An underlying theme of this Essay has been the reality of the finite, whether in terms of genetic excellence or wealth or national resource or fossil fuels. There is only just so much *stuff* to go around. The Egalitarian Fantasy, conversely, has gambled on the infinite: talent, money, resources, time. So too in terms of innovation, surely the purest expression of genetic cerebral excellence.

Look at it this way: marine construction innovations and better navigational aids literally opened up a New World of wealth seven centuries ago. Then followed agricultural and industrial technological revolutions. Following close behind were transport revolutions and then the massive exploitation of raw materials, then growth of new technologies designed for war but which came of inestimable value in peace. Commercial aviation was but one example. Growing personal wealth led to the development of vibrant financial markets, consumerism, travel and leisure.

Each of these step changes brought visible, demonstrable new waves of wealth, much of which was captured by claimants from newly emergent entrepreneurial stock. In other words, the wealth was dispersed, perhaps not quickly enough for some, but it did lead to a quantum movement forward for those many with the innate capacity to grasp the multiplicity of opportunities presented and those many others dragged along in the slip-stream of these epic social and economic changes.[1]

Next up was the digital revolution of the late 20th and early 21st Centuries. This carried with it a warning but nobody was alert to it. Unlike earlier surges of wealth and jobs created on the back of innovation, this one was muted, so much so that Alan Greenspan, Chairman of the US Federal Reserve Bank, spent much time trying to find where, exactly, lay the wealth effect of this revolution. Eventually he gave up, assuming it worked in such diffused ways that the impact was undetectable through traditional tools.[2]

We now know better. Innovation of the sort that brought mass wealth had just about reached its limits.

Because, although the digital revolution *did* create visible and enormous wealth in specific areas such as the manufacture of digital devices or the provision of search, transactional and interactional platforms, it led to old-style surges of general wealth only in developing countries where improvements in personal and innovative productivity still had the scope to spark off each other.

In developed countries the digital revolution mainly served to augment or enhance existing innovation --- or to create playthings for the idle. Put crudely, we learnt to open a car door manually, then with a key, then remotely and then by voice recognition. But the fact is, we are still only opening a car door. Here there is only marginal new wealth creation, mainly for the manufacturers, distributors and retailers of the gadgets.

We may marvel at being able to order goods online and have them delivered. But our grandparents did the same: they used the phone. Besides, if one has a limited household budget, it is irrelevant what channel one uses to buy. Again, it is of course wonderful to be able to communicate immediately with friends or to access instant information through smart phone technology. But the reality is that it is the *quality and impact* of that content which defines whether it is of value or not. Modern communication platforms degrade content through overload. A telegraph message telling you a loved one or a consignment has arrived at the port is of value. A Twitter notification to tens of thousands of arbitrary people that one's dog is ill does not. Similarly, a YouTube video of a political leader battling to eat a bacon sandwich is not information transference: it is inanity.

The digital age has thus brought convenience to the masses and efficiencies to business processes (and wealth opportunities to poor countries) but it has brought real wealth only to a comparative few in the developed world.[3] Nothing compares to the earlier forms of systemic new general wealth creation through game-changing innovation or discovery or development. Indeed, a powerful argument can be made that high end technological innovation is not improving the chances of equality in the developed world but crippling it. As the level of genetic intelligence required to access, dominate and manage this technology has risen, the pool able to service it as a proportion of the general population has shrunk.

It would be absurd to suggest that innovation as *event* has ended. Of course it has not. There will always be new discoveries, refinements, advancements and killer apps, all of which will make money for its champions and bring either entertainment or convenience to the many. But it does mean that innovation as a linear process of creating new walls of wealth and new jobs is reaching its limits. We may well have passed it.

THE PRODUCTIVITY CONUNDRUM

All of these factors have led the developed world to what could be called the productivity conundrum which lies at the heart of the inability of the developed world to get wind under its wings, to significantly lift its economies after the crash of 2008 and to provide sustainable growth paths to the future. The key lies in a concept called Total Factor Productivity.[1] This is the productivity gain brought to an economy by improvements in both human and technological efficiency.

For centuries these two had moved in tandem, leading to the great surges forward in national wealth. They still do in developing world economies which are a short distance behind the developed world on the curve, hence their robust growth. But for the last twenty years or so human productivity has been sliding backwards at an alarming rate in the developed world. Indeed, it was only productivity gains wrought by technology that prevented the true crisis from being apparent earlier.[2]

Why did human productivity decline in the West? There were five main reasons. First, the most obvious, the level of investment in productive assets fell as sensible and real money fled the home markets diminished by the economic consequences of the Egalitarian Fantasy. Second, the quality of public education in much of the developed world in the hard subjects fell in absolute terms and relative to the new comers from the East. Third, demographic change meant a growing proportion of the population was entering retirement relative to those entering the labour market. As skills are higher at point of exit rather than entrance, net productivity is affected. Fourth, the growing number of women at all levels in the work force with their propensity to retire earlier than men and to work fewer hours, affected the available skills. And, finally, whereas once the preponderance of workers were involved in real work in which they created real things for real customers at real prices, now large numbers of jobs were fantasy ones.

The linking narrative behind all these reasons for declining human productivity in the advanced economies can be summed up in three words: The Egalitarian Fantasy. The denial of the importance of genetics and biology in the formation of human talent, the refusal to tailor our post-modern societies to accommodate that reality, has led directly to the flight of investment capital, the fall in educational standards, the unsupportable generosity of pensions and the advent of supercrisis.org, all of these contributing to declining productivity.

Hordes of people were supervising, regulating, investigating, researching, hectoring, scaring, prodding or obstructing those diminishing few who were creating wealth. Millions more were pushed into positions not on the basis of their evident competence but on the basis of their gender, race or disability. Even real jobs were often devalued ones --- full-time to part-time or flexi-time, high-level to low-level, full productive day to 3.5 hour productive day, meaningful to meaningless. These fantasy jobs added little value to the economy. They were Zombie jobs, the product of six decades of the Egalitarian Fantasy. One analyst has accurately described this as *distributional* activity as opposed to *economic* activity.[3]

This led to a typically disconnected debate in the UK about why employment levels remained constant through the worst of the five-year economic slow-down after 2008. The conventional wisdom was that workers were keeping their jobs by making salary sacrifices. Partly true, but not the whole story. Wage stagnation at middle-levels had been a feature of Western economies even before the crash of 2008.

The real answer was the one that nobody wanted to address. Significant numbers of UK workers were employed in jobs that created no value anyway. So whether economic growth moved up or down was irrelevant. Their work did not constitute economic activity. Of course the advent of the zero hour contract in the UK whereby staff were retained by companies without the guarantee of hours of work, simply compounded the problem. Employment levels after 2013 were boosted but it was really a red herring. What had been multiplied was not necessarily work but work contracts, another reason aggregate wages did not rise commensurate with employment increases.

But now, unlike earlier epochs, there is no technological revolution waiting in the wings, other than perhaps some advances in medical science, energy technology and weaponry. President Obama's seed funding for a huge new project, the Brain Activity Map (BAM) announced in 2013 could be seen as the 21st Century answer to the 20th Century's Star Wars project but the scale is instructive. Star Wars cost billions of dollars and delivered trillions in terms of technological advances. BAM will initially cost $100 million. There is an added irony: the more the research progresses, the greater will be our understanding of the fatal misunderstandings of human nature that underpin the post-modern world, the more we will grasp the flaws in the Egalitarian Fantasy.

It can come as no surprise, then, that by 2012 the Total Factor Productivity had dropped to 1970 levels in the US.[4] And that was the best in the developed world, bar some North European economies. The UK, once the most productive country in the world, had by 2014 become the least productive of the G7 Group of nations. Forty years of rising growth in the productivity rate wiped out in five years, thanks to the cumulative effects of the Egalitarian Fantasy.

This worrying decline in total factor productivity has been camouflaged for years for three reasons. Firstly, wages have been declining, thus pushing nominal per capita productivity. Secondly, declining numbers of people in employment shoved up the productivity of those remaining in work. Thirdly, technological changes ratcheted up the productivity of the work force as a whole. None of this, of course, was due to an appreciable improvement in the productivity of the individual. Institutions like the International Labour Organisation persistently argued that labour productivity was rising as wages declined, another charge against the capitalist system, without acknowledging the accompanying factors.

It is in this context that one must seek to understand the current existential crises of the developed world: political, economic, social and geo-strategic. For 60 years the developed world had spent considerable wealth in seeking to develop those at the lowest levels of the society with little appreciable result in terms of economic growth. The chimera of full equality had so deluded Western elites that they have committed us to senseless, dangerous and ideological courses of action.

In doing so the developed world triggered unintended consequences which undercut its wealth-creating capacity, raised unsustainable debt, pauperized culture and heightened public expectations to polarizing levels. As real jobs fled, the Egalitarian Fantasy was forced to create fantasy ones in the bureaucracies and in super-crisis.org; jobs and functions that further crippled the economic vigour of developed world countries and drove more job losses. It became a downward spiral. In every case, the Egalitarian Fantasy brought stagnation for the majority, deterioration for the minority and extreme wealth for a few. It has achieved the opposite of its intention.

THE EGALITARIAN FANTASY FEEDS THE GROWTH OF INEQUALITY

The extent to which the egalitarian project has failed in its prime objective of reducing inequality has been camouflaged down the decades by the fact that aggregate incomes rose and material accumulation increased, much of this through direct wealth transfers to the lower socio-economic groups.   All the boats rose in the harbour as economies grew, but some rose much faster than others. Also, the routine ascendancy of 10% of the lowest quintile to a higher level every generation, except the last, yielded enough individual success stories to divert attention from the 90% who were severely limited in their prospects of advancement.

In reality, income inequality within developed countries was widening[1], life expectancies diverging,[2] physical and mental capacities between the forward groups and the hindmost ones were growing steadily and dangerously apart. The reason was obvious. As the Egalitarian Fantasy drove swathes of low and lower middle level jobs abroad, the ones left behind were either the very high-skilled ones, the very low-skilled ones or the fantasy ones.

The individuals poised to take advantage of this globalisation dividend were the ones who possessed the innate propensity and the non-cognitive character to seize opportunity. They were the ones who largely through private wealth and education had generationally stayed aloof from the carnage wrought by the Egalitarian Fantasy on public education for the less wealthy.[3] The Devil, however, was taking the hindmost. Research by Oxford University and published in *The British Journal of Sociology* in 2014[4] showed that for the first time in history the middle classes were falling further down the socio-economic ladder: downward mobility was growing faster than upward mobility.

The gap in income between a magic success class and the rest had become excessive by 2012. The share of income of the top one per cent of Americans, for example, had risen to 19.6%. It had never been above 10% from the end of World War ll until the mid-1980's. Then globalization and its opportunities for enrichment swept up the top end ... just as the consequences of The Egalitarian Fantasy began sweeping away the lower end.

This significant difference in wealth acquisition was of course immediately seized upon by the Egalitarian Fantasists to argue the failure of market economies and advance the old chestnut that equal societies are more successful than unequal ones. Others argued that wealth would always outstrip income, thus ensuring that inequality must grow through capitalism.[5]. Both propositions were based on a flawed analysis of the problem: they ignored the critical importance of genetic capacity.

Growing inequality was a direct consequence of an Egalitarian Fantasy that had destroyed the manufacturing sectors in the developed world thus obliterating tens of millions of low and middle level jobs, removed opportunities for investment and driven intellectual property, investors and high-level entrepreneurial talent into other pursuits --- like the financial sector where they could earn multiples better than in manufacturing. It was also the Egalitarian Fantasy that depressed educational standards for the lower groups and turned many of them into dependency cases.

It was also not by chance that the society with the most pervasive, albeit not necessarily most generous, welfare systems, the UK and the USA for example, suffered the greatest gaps in skills levels between highest and lowest and this coincided with class.[6] The countries with more focused welfare systems and a sharper drive for excellence in education, such as the Scandinavian societies, showed comparatively less of a divide and less association with class.

The argument that egalitarian societies are more successful, therefore egalitarianism makes for success, is in any case a classic *a priori* argument. Scandinavian countries had the genetic predisposition towards success and were largely homogenous and equal to begin with, which is why they became successful. Nigeria (as opposed to the many individual Nigerian success stories amongst this most enterprising of communities) has neither a national disposition towards success nor is it homogenous or equal, which is why it is struggling to be successful as a country. There is no rocket science here.

The Egalitarian Fantasy also drove away entrepreneurs and aspirers through its relentless denigration of wealth and success. Unsurprisingly, the wealth-creating elites had become more impatient and contemptuous of the lower socio-economic groups and sought to keep as much of their wealth as possible, hence the furious political fights about tax evasion by individuals and corporations bitterly opposed to the fact that an ever smaller group of personal and corporate taxpayers in the developed world are carrying an ever heavier burden of the tax.

In 1986, the top 10% of US federal taxpayers paid 54.6% of the taxes and the other 90% paid 45.3%. By 2013, the top 10% were paying 70.6% and the rest 29.4%.[7] The Egalitarian Fantasy had ensured that even as the lower earners were absolved of ever greater tax responsibilities, the middle and top earners were picking up the tab.

Across major airports in the developed world bonded warehouses were built for the storage of articles of extremely high value for the rich --- wine, art, jewellery. Again, the development of virtual currencies, modelled on Bitcoin, holds the promise, once past its obvious current shortcomings, of being the first stage in the creation of a private global currency for the super rich, immune to the political manipulations of national currencies and not subject to the behest and interests of politicians operating on behalf of the wealth consuming classes.

How long will it be before banking itself will become the prerogative of the very rich, the rest of us dependent either on state financing or on the corner money lenders who through European history have exacted high returns for their loans and dread penalties for default ? Or will banks themselves become redundant as new means of digital transacting create all sorts of opportunities for entrepreneurs? Whatever, these wealth creators are becoming more mobile, taking themselves, their wealth-creating bloodlines and their capital to countries where they feel less oppressed, or at least less irritated. The consuming groups, meanwhile, become more isolated, querulous, demanding …. and dependent.

Here then the supreme irony. In the face of the increasing depredations by governments to raise the money to fund the Egalitarian Fantasy, the rich are reverting to Medieval ways of protecting their assets and the poor are more exposed than ever. It is a sad indictment of how fractured the developed world has become as a result of the social and economic deformations created by The Egalitarian Fantasy. Everywhere the evidence of growing disparities in lifestyles and expectations is growing.

A report by the UK's Institute for Fiscal Studies in January 2015 found that while all wages had fallen in real terms during the recession, it was the top and middle earners who had taken the real pain relative to the lower earners: a 7.2% fall at the top versus 5.6% at the bottom.[8] A legitimate argument can be made that the poor suffer more in absolute terms than the rich because their disposable income is so much smaller but it cannot alter the fact that the burden of loss has fallen heaviest at the top and middle, nor could it camouflage the fact that a shrinking number of taxpayers are carrying the load. And they were not happy.

Intriguing research by statistician Simon Briscoe in the UK in early 2015 revealed the disconcerting fact that while average wages had fallen, the real wages of people in employment for longer than a year had actually risen. So the gap between the richest and the poorest was being compounded by a gap between those in formal and regular employment and those outside it. Inequality was no longer simply a function of absolute wealth but now also of relative wealth.

In some parts of major British cities the life expectancies between one neighbourhood and another is 10 years.[9] It was in these cities that the British socialists had taken great pride in the destruction of historic neighbourhoods where once poor people lived in old, dilapidated, squalid homes with outside loos: indeed they destroyed more of these homes than the Luftwaffe in the Blitz.

Instead of restoring and modernizing these historic old neighbourhoods, they dispersed the inhabitants to new estate homes with *inside* loos, homes which soon became dilapidated and squalid and something the old homes had not been --- dangerous and soulless. Where once communities could observe and keep control of their children at street level, now the parents sat in soulless high-rise blocks and their children were yielded unseen to the parks and backstreets. Like all true Stalinists, the socialists preferred to measure progress by the cold logic of bricks and mortar and money rather than the softer issues of community, family, tradition and a sense of belonging.

In the UK, the socialist government of Gordon Brown took pride in claiming it had lifted 750 000 children "out of poverty", largely by extensions of tax credits, thus creating notional value. It had done no such thing of course and it required a sober assessment a year into the life of the successor government to find that there had been virtually no improvement in any of the key lifestyle indicators for the recipients. The money spent could be considered wasted.[10]. In reality, what had happened with the real cash that did come though, was a priming of lower-income households' consumption spending through transfers from the state, nearly all of which went on consumer goods and very little on long term investment in wealth, health, education or environment.

Behind this so-called progress, of course, the lower end of the traditional working class was tumbling into crisis physically, emotionally, intellectually and numerically. The BBC's 2013 Great British Class Survey estimated that the core working class component in the UK had fallen to 14% and was "fading from contemporary importance". In its place had arisen a "precariat", a 15% slice of the population drifting between state hand-outs and low-level work.[11] Remarkably, in the United States this proportion of the population in the "underclass" is almost the same.

Falling standards of education and public health care, partly a function of unionisation (historically, trade unions have been the pillaging pike men of the Egalitarian Fantasy, although ironically representing a labour elite) and lack of intellectual resources, left the lower groups imperfectly equipped to take advantage of even the low-level jobs that existed.[12]

The welfare state encouraged dependency and destroyed one of the most important drivers of human progress --- *physical mobility.* The course of human success is ineluctably tied to the concept of mobility. People historically moved on when the crops failed or the livestock died from diseases, when jobs in one sector closed, when a town faded, when a national economy faltered, when vast new territories opened up for settlement, when industries relocated; when any of this happened people physically shifted and created new and in most cases better lives.

The welfare state cut off this path to opportunity for the poor at a stroke. Why move when you could stay where you were on benefits? Once your home was where your heart was. Now it was where your benefits payment was made.

As the levels of benefits rose, so did the social pathologies: substance abuse, domestic violence and obesity, so much so that obesity by 2012 was considered an illness of the poor, something incomprehensible in developing world countries and that would be inexplicable to a Victorian.[13]

The post war dream of creating a social welfare system that would progressively narrow inequalities within developed world countries was thus rocked back on its heels. The gap between success groups and left behind groups grew within developed countries, even as inequalities narrowed between high-potential developing countries like China and India, on the one hand, and the developed world countries, on the other.

A seminal research project by an economist Gregory Clark in 2013, sought to track the social migration of individuals and groups in six countries through analysis of the fortunes of families with rare surnames during three centuries.[14] The result: social migration is slow and has remained so despite all and every social intervention in history. His models suggest it would take between ten and fifteen generations for either elites or the lowest groups to socially migrate to the norm. Astonishingly, he finds that levels of social migration in the England of the Middle Ages were greater than those in contemporary Britain.

And there is another factor affecting the quest for this elusive "equality". The science of DNA full sequence scanning has reached such a stage that it is now possible to scan, at comparatively little cost, for 3 200 genetic deficiencies in an unborn foetus. The scans overwhelmingly focus on detecting congenital illness but can also scan markers for cognitive and non cognitive competence.

By 2014 three major international research projects were underway into determining the role of genes in the formation of the human body and mind. In the US, a huge project to map the human mind (MAP) was launched in 2013. In the UK more than 100 000 genomes were involved in research to detect early markers for cancer. The Daily Telegraph's Science writer predicted in 2015 that in twenty years, chemotherapy would be dead. Genetic interventions would cure cancer. And again in the US, the Genomic Psychiatric Project, involving hundreds of research partners, sought more clearly to identify the genetic basis of a range of serious psychiatric disorders.

With this wealth of new data rolling into the public domain, it was inevitable that the world's elites would be interested. After all, they have since the origin of species historically selected mates for best characteristics of progeny. Now they have science at their disposal. As the cost of rearing children grows, the temptation of the wealth and success classes and nations to pre-select their children according to winner genotype will be overwhelming.

The result can only be smaller but more gifted elites set amongst a rapidly growing pool of people living longer. Some analysts believe this magic circle will be no more than 15% of the population in developed societies and will consist of those with the inherent capacity to exploit new technologies. The other 85%, those outside this magic ring, face being replaced by the technologies.[15]

And what will those other 85% do for a living ? What many of them are already doing, earning a crust from working in the "caring" industries, creating and expanding crises and victims so as to justify employment or being recipients of charity. Already, the normalisation of a clearly abnormal situation in the developed world is underway. Some protagonists of supercrisis.org are suggesting it is the natural order of things in the 21st century state for a small percentage of the population to be creating the wealth so that others can be employed in altruistic service with the rest relying on subsidy. It is a fatal argument and a grim prospect for three reasons.

First, it accepts the end of western manufacturing capacity as a fiat accompli and thus turns negligence into a virtue; second, it ignores the fact that the entrenchment of supercrisis.org ensures the further erosion of western competitiveness thus turning defeat into desirability, and third, it converts independence into dependence for huge numbers of people.

This idea of islands of excellence within seas of mediocrity is not in the realm of supposition. Recent research indicates that reaction times --- a key component of genetic intelligence --- are on average slower amongst 21st Century people in the developed world than in Victorian times.[16] Other research in 2012 by the Organisation for Economic Co-operation and Development (OECD) showed that educational standards in the current school-going generation were hardly better than in their grand-parent's generation --- and in the UK's case they were worse.[17]

Studies by the University of Australia in 2013, meanwhile, found that modern children would finish a minute and a half --- or 300 yards --- behind children of 1975 in a one mile race.[18] Rising average pulse rates amongst children aged nine to 11 in the developed world through the 25 years to 2012 --- two beats per minutes for boys and one for girls --- spoke of increasingly unhealthy lifestyles.[19]. Research by the UK's

National Trust in 2014, found that children in the 7-12 age group were spending only a third of the time outdoors compared to their grandparents, less than an hour a day. The rest was spent in front of television sets and computers, ensnared by social media.[20] Public Health England meanwhile confirmed in 2014 that the incidence of sexual diseases in children in the UK had doubled in a decade.

Some societies, like Britain's, were becoming so somnambulant that in the 50 years prior to 2013, physical activity levels amongst adults as measured by metabolic equivalent task units had declined 20% and by 2030 daily activity levels would be barely 25% above people who spent the whole day in bed.[21]

What cause these doleful statistics, this deterioration of average levels of mental and physical health amongst humans in the richest countries in the world? Those components of the developed world population that are the most dependent on the support of others are growing faster than the portion that is the opposite, thanks to the welfare state and modern medicine.[22] All but a few boats in the harbour are now falling.

The scale of the problem at the lowest level is not hard to determine. The United Kingdom, purely by way of example, has identified 120 000 "problem" households which account for a considerable amount of the state's investment in response actions, counselling, prosecuting, remedial educating, medicating, nursing and instructing --- at an average rate of nearly £900 000 per household per generation.[23]

Falling levels of crime in developed world societies, meanwhile, have been matched by a new phenomenon: the increasing role played by the repeat offender. By 2013, up to a third of criminals were repeat offenders with as many as 15 previous convictions.[24] London Metropolitan Police statistics released in early 2015 showed that of the 3 914 people convicted or cautioned during the August 2011 riots in the UK, 1593 had reoffended less than three years after being released. Vast investment in counselling and rehabilitation had clearly failed, so it is reasonable to assume that this group of reoffenders represent the core of those innately predisposed to crime.

Indeed, research by Sweden's Karolinska Institute has established the intriguing fact that siblings born into families only recently emerged from poverty have no difference in incidences of criminality than their older siblings who were born into poverty -- a clear indication that crime has a significant, perhaps determining, genetic component.[25] Other research showed this class of repeat offender invariably had material deformations of the of the brain. In the case of criminals it was a shrunken

centromedial prefrontal cortex and in habitual criminals it was an under-developed dorsolateral prefrontal
cortex.[26]

The mounting scientific evidence posed an acute
dilemma for the Egalitarian Fantasists in the fields of
penology and criminology. What once appeared so
simple – poverty and childhood misfortune causes
crime --- becomes entirely something else if habitual criminality is in fact a function of chemicals and
brain formation. What are the options? Genetic editing? Indefinite incarceration? Sterilisation ? Same old
same old? I will not presume to make a recommenda-
tion, but it is an astonishing testimony to the crushing
power of the Egalitarian Fantasy and Groupthink that
there is no serious debate in the ranks of professional
criminologists and penologists on the implications of
recent scientific discoveries about the genetic and biological basis of habitual criminality.

SUMMARY SO FAR

*Post Second World War social, political and economic formations
have been based on the scientifically erroneous assumption that
all humans are genetically and biologically equal and can rise
equally to opportunity and changed circumstances. This flawed*

assumption has been kept alive by the powerful vested interests of the Left, despite decades of mounting empirical and scientific counter evidence.

In pursuit of the chimera of complete equality, the developed world has misallocated excessive national resources towards unproductive sectors of the society at the cost of its overall human and physical infrastructure. This in turn has exacerbated the developed world's loss of competitive advantage against new comers.

The immediate effect of this has been the migration of middle and low level jobs to developing world countries. This has directly brought about the creation of tens of millions of superfluous jobs in the governmental and neo-governmental sectors, the quangos and charities, to hide the fact that many real jobs have evaporated. This "fantasy job" sector has created no wealth, indeed the reverse. It has distorted rational economic and human activity to such an extent that it has engineered a profound crisis of identity, integrity, trust and confidence amongst developed world societies.

Worse, the decades-long support of the Egalitarian Fantasy by western governments has led to the accrual of unsustainable levels of debt. All of this came to a head when a rapacious banking sector precipitated the 2008 GFC, or Great Financial Crisis, a direct consequence of unsustainable levels of debt and precipitated by ideologically driven egalitarian policies in the US housing market.

The developed world was at last confronted by the terrible realization that wealth is finite --- one cannot take more out of a closed system than one puts in, other than by fabricating notional wealth through monetary and financial engineering, enterprises which we know always have long tail negative effects. There is also a glimmering awareness that the quantum of human genetic capacity might also be finite in a world of ever-increasing demand for intellectual virtuosity. This poses a great future challenge. As advances in biomedicine prolong human life and expand population numbers, a diminishing proportion of the population in the developed world will be sufficiently equipped to create the wealth and provide the resources needed for the many to live even subsistence existences.

Our only options then are to engineer excellence through genetic modification or to improve our capacity to identify and develop genetic excellence wherever it occurs within our societies. I have already argued that the genetic modification of humans is now and probably for some time to come, a step too far. But management of our existing genetic stock is within our grasp. Others are already doing it. It is not by chance that significant chunks of Chinese national resources are devoted to detecting and promoting excellence within their populations. Additionally, it is not coincidental that Chinese people are in terms of quality and representation in the forefront of those geneticists delving ever deeper into the nature of our very being, nor is it by chance that the largest gene sequencing facility in the world, BGI, is located in Shenzhen in China and it is not surprising that in 2015 China's Sun Yatsen University in Guangzhou was the first to publicly admit it was attempting to apply the CRISPR/Cas9 process to create *genetically modified human embryos, thus unleashing a world wide frenzy of ethical debate.*

We can now turn to considering the Egalitarian Fantasy's impact on developed world politics and in particular on gender, immigration and cultural issues. In the last part, we will look at how all of this has affected the status of the developed world in the 21ˢᵗ Century.

THE FEMINIST FRANCHISE

Undoubtedly, the most important social development in the 20ᵗʰ century was the empowerment of women. A number of sequential factors stood behind this revolution: the Enlightenment, improved availability of education, changing legal regimes, structural changes in the labour market brought on initially by World Wars but subsequently entrenched, advances in birth control methods, popular media, travel opportunities and so endlessly on.

This changed role of women in the modern world has been overwhelmingly beneficial to the individual and the society. It has made available new pools of genetic talent to the business and financial world, serviced growing economies, gentled politics and led to a greater sense of empathy in national policy making, although there are those who would argue that the latter has made western governance less effective and thus more vulnerable.

It has also had a profound effect on the advancement of human capacity: the research indicates that the average IQ of women in the developed world is now for the first time equal to men. The mere engagement with modernity in the business, working and professional world in developed economies has improved IQ levels among women.[1]

But if so much is right, why is so much wrong ?

The answer tracks back to the old culprit: the Egalitarian Fantasy and in particular the Feminist Franchise of super-cisis.org. It is this franchise that has taken everything that is important and necessary in this social revolution and converted it into an ideological cause demanding extremist methods and absurd ends. In so doing, the extremist feminists have flown in the face of biological and genetic reality with grave consequences for all. Ironically, their very extremism has undermined their own cause.

In pursuit of a complete equality of women with men, it has achieved the opposite. Women have been elevated from being part of our species to something above it: protected, exceptional, untouchable, incapable of making their own decisions, not responsible for their actions. Supported by the crassest of commercial interests and the most mindless pandering of modern media, the extreme feminists, particularly in the legal, political and academic world, have done more to objectify, patronise and infantilise modern women then the worst of Victorian patriarchs.

This essay will argue that an already vigorous and successful social evolution which was organically delivering great and lasting benefit to society was side tracked into a dangerous revolution to force ideological and statistical equality, irrespective of the consequences. Those consequences, it will be suggested, have been material: the trapping of large numbers of disillusioned single mothers into juggling career and caring; the repression of middle-class wages; the exacerbation of existing household inequality; the economic marginalization of huge numbers of lower income women; the distortion of relationships between the sexes; the further erosion of the family and, via abortion and delayed child birth, a reproductive failure to match society's need to sustain itself, the deepening of social pathologies in the youth; the perversion of legal processes and last, but not least, it has laid the foundations for a future crisis in high level skills availability.

The impact of the Feminist Franchise was different according to the socio-economic and skills levels of its target group. Thus middle to upper class women took from feminism that which suited them. They rightly insisted on equal opportunities at work, equality at law, in the home and in control of their own bodies. They also sought equal pay for what were often unequal contributions of labour.[2] But they carefully ignored the extremist forms of feminism which did not serve their interests. Thus they still sought long term partners able to provide for them and their children when they no longer worked; fulfilment of the most elemental biological instinct. They married later and longer, divorced less and had a greater proportion of children within wedlock.[3]

There was of course a price to be paid by the society as a whole for this civilized and egalitarian arrangement. Statistically, one third of working professional mothers will take between one and three years off from their careers to raise children. Two thirds will by choice end up either taking early retirement or working part-time.[4]. Women will on average take 50% more time off from work than men --- often to care for a dependent. It does not require the greatest analytical skill to determine that the more one increases for ideological reasons the employment of a particular group that is demonstrably working less than another one, overall productivity is going to take a sizeable knock.

A swatch of recent research is indicating that many women would prefer not to work at all. Sixty per cent said in a 2014 UK survey that they would leave work immediately if they could afford to do so.[5] The corresponding number for men is not available but in would most certainly be far less than for women.[6]. There is thus a contradiction between the claim on the one hand that women are held back at work by discrimination against them *as* women and, on the other hand, the statistical fact that the majority put in less work hours, days, months and years than men and that the majority of women would stop work altogether if they could. The net effect of all this downtime relative to males in economic terms is a much lower return on investment in the high-level training of women.[7] Again, there is no moral issue here. It is simple economics.

Only now are professional organisations waking up to the fact that the egalitarian promotion of women candidates for places at things like medical schools (nearly 50% by 2014 in the UK) can only lead to a crisis of supply of qualified professionals down the road when up to 30% of them per graduate year decamp for early retirement or part-time work.[8] This leads to its own set of problems. Who is to replace them? Men? No chance: they already work longer years, hours and weeks than their women counterparts; they die earlier and endure more stress[9]. Foreign imports? There are huge practical and political problems to this as the UK began discovering as it sought to bolster its ailing and egalitarian national health service.[10]

Something will have to give. Either the society will have to accept the cost of ideological investments in high-level skills training for women or women will have to renounce their biological evolutionary instincts, what is called their "parental investment".[11] As the developed world will have increasingly fewer resources for the former, and women show no inclination to the latter, crisis, a real and not fantasy one, looms in the high level skills availability in the future for the developed world.

But perhaps the most important unintended consequence in the feminist project has been on income inequality. The growth of new streams of highly educated and well paid women has seen an exponential growth in household incomes at the top of the scale. In 1960, 25% of men with university degrees married women with degrees: there were just not enough degreed women about. By 2005, it was 48% and rising.

The net effect of two high earners on household income and the Gini coefficient, the scale that measures inequality within a society is apparent. In 1960 it was 0.34 and by 2005 was 0.43, a large part of this driven by the two-person, high-earner household. So here, as in so much else, was a clear example of the mutually exclusive goals of egalitarianism. One could not encourage the professional advancement of women and simultaneously expect a reduction in household income inequality.

So much for the high-flyers. What about the middle classes? The feminist project also had its unintended consequences here. The mass advent of women to the working world after World War ll coincided with a structural change in the developed world's labour markets.

Manufacturing industry, except in certain high level sectors, decamped to the developing world as a direct consequence of the Egalitarian Fantasy's inflation of the social cost of labour, a theme discussed earlier in this Essay. Male workers who had excelled in this area faced redundancy. Historically, such people have migrated to work in new sectors. But that was no longer possible. So that left the booming services sector: financial institutions, customer care, retail and, of course, the supercrisis.org franchises.

But here's the rub: these posts had rapidly been filled either by women, who often proved better and more adaptable to the demands of these sectors, or foreigners, many not even living in the host countries thanks to the miracle of modern call centres. This not only meant working class and lower middle class men found it difficult to get jobs, but it ensured the depression of wages across the whole sector because of the abundance of middle to low level labour: a recent feature of all developed countries.

The statistics tell the story in the number of women comprising the prime working members of households (now above 40% in the UK) and the disproportionate number of women taken on in new job creation in recent years in, say, the UK (almost 15 females to one male).[12]

An added factor was the deliberate adoption of taxation regimes by socialist and left-wing governments throughout the developed world which penalized married couples. Patricia Morgan, a British sociologist specializing in family policy, records in her *Farewell To The Family (1999),* the grim statistics.

In England in the 1950's a married father of two children had to earn 101% of average manual wages before he qualified for tax. By 1999 he entered the tax regime at 35% of manual earnings. In 1948, the average US family paid two per cent in tax. By 1999 it was 24% in Federal taxes and up to 10% in local taxes. Exemptions to married families that once applied to 42% of average family earnings, 60 years later applied to 12%.

The consequence of all this was the end of the single household bread-winner. The depression of wages (by 2012 one in three workers in the 16 to 30 year bracket were considered low wage compared to one in five in the 1970's, according to the UK Office for National Statistics) and the high levels of taxation, ensured that both parents *had* to work or the household *had* to rely on state patronage. Either way, it was the death of the self-sufficient, single male earner household and a huge impairment to the traditional and biological care-giving and nurturing role of the woman, a role which swathes of recent research indicate a majority of women welcome.

It had another unintended and baleful consequence. Statistically, both men and women in postmodern society have been having children later in life. The UK's Office for National Statistics reported in 2014 that the average age of first time British mothers was 30 years --- four years older than five years earlier. The reasons are not hard to find. Women delay having children so as to continue providing a second household income. This is particularly important because of the highly unstable nature of contemporary relationships, a direct function of the destruction of core traditional family values in the developed world. Men, who invariably end up supporting children in non-welfare households after the women retire early or take part-time work, in turn delay having children so as to accumulate as much wealth as possible.

The British Pregnancy Advisory Service reported in 2014 that the fertility rate for women over 40 years of age had trebled since 1991. But recent research shows that children of older parents have a far higher incidence of brain dysfunction compared to those of younger parents. The University of California Davis's Health Systems research, published in the Live Science February 8 2010 edition, reported that mothers birthing over 40 years of age had a 50% higher chance of having an autistic child than a mother between 25 and 29. The legacy of the feminist franchise of the Egalitarian Fantasy will thus live on --- long after our societies return to biological and genetic reality.

The consequences of this headlong surge of women into the business world, propelled at dangerous velocity by industrialization and spurred on by the feminist project, were captured in a 2014 report by Project 28-40 by Opportunity Now, described as an organisation that campaigns for gender equality. It surveyed 25 000 UK women aged 28 to 40 and found that the concept of flexible working time was failing and causing tensions between professional and career women, on the one hand, and flexitime mothers, on the other.

The former felt they had to pick up the slack for the latter. The survey found that the majority of women believed flexitime indicated a "less committed" attitude on the part of the employee and that it was a real barrier to career progression. Instinctively, the report blames businesses and managers for not being "creative" in their flexitime structures.

The conclusion is of course misguided. Flexitime is inherently and unavoidably unproductive in terms of continuity, co-ordination, management and focus. That is a simple fact, as anybody who has been in business knows. Part-time work, no matter how useful, does not equal in value or productivity full time work. There is no way to fix it. But it did reinforce what reams of other research had been revealing. Most women do not want to work at all, women are stressed about trying to perform at work and maintain households and many feel under pressure by being "overloaded" with work or subject to constant criticism.

This profound conflict between biological and ideological imperative, not surprisingly, is taking a heavy toll on high level women achievers. Nearly a third of women CEO's in the top companies were asked to step down in the decade prior to 2014. The comparative number for men was a quarter. Thirty five per cent of women who made it to the top were from outside the company. Only 22% of men were.[13] As insiders have a statistically better track record of achievement than outsiders, it is not difficult to see why women have a lower success rate than men at the very top.

Why this lack of in-house candidates? Affirmative action pressures have prompted companies to hire female outsiders rather than male insiders. To find out why there are insufficient suitable women insiders we have to go to other pieces of illuminating research which showed that women were mentored in senior positions more than men, despite the fact that the majority of women in senior positions did not ask for mentoring at all. The reason was that many feared that by asking they may appear insecure or incompetent, thus reinforcing the stereotyping they had fought so hard to avoid. Even when they did get support, suggests some research, it was the wrong kind: mentorship as opposed to sponsorship.[14] The distinction may appear illusory but it is not: the former equips somebody to understand the technicalities of the business; the latter inducts, guides and introduces them to the processes which lead to promotion.

The research would suggest senior male executives are happy to extend mentorship but not sponsorship as they do to male aspirants. So why are women in senior positions being "over-mentored and under-sponsored", in the words of a Harvard Business Review article? A host of reasons are advanced except the most obvious: senior males are concerned about close association with younger female colleagues for fear of being accused of nepotism by others or, worse, charged with sexual discrimination when the mentee fails, something that is rife in western business thanks to the work of extremist feminism. The very aggressiveness of the late 20th century variant of feminism has thus undermined its own cause.

An even more ominous development was to be found not at the level of senior corporate life but at the most elemental level of all: primary and secondary education. By 2014, males had almost entirely deserted education as a field of employment. In the UK, merely for example, 97% of teachers in lower and secondary education were female. The reason? Amongst others, males felt themselves vulnerable to harassment charges by girl students. One can take various views on this but a society which has succeeded in almost entirely intimidating its male component out of the education of its young, is in for long term trouble.

The push effect of the feminist franchise of the Egalitarian Fantasy and the pull effect of growing economies drew huge numbers of women into work in the first waves of "liberation". Now they confronted reality --- and biology. The majority preferred not being employed and had no long term intention to remain employed. Many felt unequal to its rigours. They would rather be mothers at home and have male partners putting a crust on the table.

But events had moved on too fast. The Egalitarian Fantasy had rewritten the rules. First, middle and lower level wages were depressed because of the flood of women employees and the exodus of such jobs abroad so households could no longer rely solely on the wages of a male partner, other than in exceptional circumstances and, second, there were a limited number of such long haul partners around --- a permissive environment had helped destroy the institution of marriage and impaired even long-term relationships.

But the extremist feminist project had its direst impact at the lower level of developed world societies, roughly the bottom quintile on the scale of socio-economic status. Women in these groups, bereft of the sort of nuanced selectivity shown by the higher groups in embracing the project, simply bought the whole leftist feminist package. As an expression of "independence", many became recklessly pregnant and then at a great rate as the welfare system rewarded irresponsibility and their access to the job market brought independent incomes, albeit pitifully low. They married less, divorced sooner and had more subsidised children out of wedlock.

So independent did they become that they initiated divorce against men at a rate three times that of men against women.[15] Between 1970 and 2011, the cause for separations due to the "unreasonable behaviour" of the women partner increased six fold in the UK.[16] The massive expansion of the legal framework, as discussed above, hardly helped.

In divorce settlements, meanwhile, men faced systemic discrimination through the courts in rights of access to children and through their employers in terms of requests for the flexitime to care for their children --- men were twice as likely to be refused flexitime as women[17] Whatever benefits this Franchise of the Egalitarian Fantasy had bought to women had thus come at a cost to stable unions and to the principle fairness between males and females, particularly amongst the lower socio-economic groups.

The powerful stabilising effect of marriage and two-parent households was blown to pieces.[18]. In the United States, for example, only six per cent of college graduates have children out of wedlock. Forty four per cent of high school graduates and 67% of school drop-outs do, the largest gap since these records were kept.[19] The consequence of the destruction of this stabilizing element in society has been profound: More than 70% of the children admitted to local authority care in the UK come from broken homes. Children from broken homes are two or three times more likely to be suspended from school. One in five children in the UK live with their biological father. Step fathers, meanwhile, are 14 times more likely than biological fathers to abuse their children.[20].

Across the developed world households with single female parents were consistently rated as the most impoverished in the society with their children falling distressingly amongst the most "at risk". Research by the US-based *Home Observation for Measurement of the Environment (HOME scale)* in 2014 revealed that 44% of the women who were ranked amongst the bottom 25% in terms of parenting skills, were single mothers.

Here, then, was the inevitable conclusion of the extremist feminist strain of the Egalitarian Fantasy and its irresponsible promises of an undefined and utopian "liberation". Women without the capacity for discerning the reality from the fantasy bought the feminist package in its entirety and ended up living without partner support, no hope of reasonable employment and diminishing state subsidy.

The UK Insolvency Services report of 2013 found that women in 18 to 24 year age group were twice as likely to be insolvent as their male peers. Only the extension of debt relief orders, which allowed debt to be written off, prevented it from being worse. As these young women struggled to earn enough to survive through dead-end jobs, care of the children was ceded to the television screen, the play station and the streets.

The consequence is to be found in the disturbingly high rise in social pathologies amongst the young of the lower socio-economic groups, particularly in the Anglo-Saxon world where these trends have not been mitigated by the power of faith, family and duty as they have been in many other developed societies in Europe.

Despite this mass of empirical evidence showing the consequence of the break-up of traditional family units in the developed world, there still exists at virtually every level of policy-making and administration, those who would seek to deny the obvious, one, Lord Wilson of Culworthy, a High Court Justice, even coining the repulsively anodyne term "blended family" to describe the circumstances in which children are compelled to live in households in which one partner is not a biological parent and where merely by statistical probability they are going to have a lousier time than if they had been in a stable family environment in their formative years.

And this feminist tradition had another impact: the unwillingness of children raised in the welfare state to take care of aged parents. That charge fell to the welfare state which, of course, failed.[21] In the UK, the number of people living alone doubled in the decade between 2003 and 2013, a rate of increase ten-fold that of the average population increase. The immediate cause: people marrying later, divorcing more often and living longer.[22]

But there was another and more profound reason. The deformation of ordinary human relations by the strictures imposed by the seared and blasted extremist feminist view of human nature, embedded and embraced in academia, the public service and the legal system, had persuaded many people that it was just not worth engaging the opposite sex other than on the most fleeting, indeed primeval, terms.

And so much of the Anglo Saxon world started exhibiting the most tragic of all social phenomena. Groups of aging men alone or looking for the company of other men in the bars or public places or sporting associations. And even larger formations of lone women locked into barren and misanthropic social groups, listening endlessly to each other's tales of male betrayal and perfidy.

Worse, the very notion of innately embedded differences in the aptitudes between the sexes, differences now soundly established by science, is under attack by the feminists and their cohorts. In its endless quest to redefine the crisis so as to keep crisis alive, the feminist franchise of supercrisis.org has moved beyond a demand for female equality --- that has been achieved in the west in every sense that is within the gift of humans to offer. Now it is an attempt to destroy the concept of gender differentiation itself. Its most absurd manifestation is the obsession with gender neutral colours: hard times are ahead for blues and pinks. Less amusing, is the attack on literature to comply with this androgynous new world, a subject dealt with more fully later in this Essay. A full-blown new victim sub franchise has grown up around what is called gender identity politics: a bizarre and arcane world of transgender rows and tiffs, not worthy of further consideration in this Essay. Suffice it to say that all these divisions will be humbled by the implacable forces of biology and genes. But before then, as always, lie heart breaking social confusion, dislocation and disillusionment.

And none of this revolution appears to have altered the fundamentals. Despite the most generous and accommodating social and economic policies, women's penetration to the highest levels of the big corporations is still low. A slew of data now available from research into women's progress in Scandinavian countries, the most active and earliest in promoting the interests of women, raises serious doubts about the premise of post-modern feminism.

Although many Scandinavian countries had imposed quotas for women board members of up to 40%, less than six per cent of CEO positions in 2014 were occupied by women --- hardly better than the five per cent in the USA with no such quotas. Denmark, with no quotas, had the same proportion of women in top positions as Norway, which had. Despite this clear indication of the lack of correlation between board membership and executive leadership, Germany in 2014 followed with legislation compelling 30% representation of women on boards. It was pure tokenism and it is difficult to judge which is the more offensive, the pusillanimous politicians who legislated it, supercrisis.org bureaucrats who drove it or the broad mass of women who meekly acquiesced in this insulting patronisation.

Other research yielded the intriguing possibility that it was precisely the generosity of the welfare state in Scandinavian countries that was hampering the advancement of women. The attraction of bountiful maternity provisions, for example, persuaded many women to have children early in their careers, precisely when according to the feminist mantra they should have been advancing at work and consolidating their positions.[23] The gap was taken by their male counterparts. When offered equal parental leave policies as their female partners through legislative changes in the UK in 2014, the response by males was underwhelming. Preliminary surveys indicated that only between two and six per cent of those eligible would take up the opportunity. Why? They were afraid of falling off the ladder and intuitively feared that the burden for financially providing for hearth and home would be theirs in the future.

Other research in Scandinavian countries indicated that the high levels of taxation in these countries to pay for these social policies left less disposable income for domestic help for working women --- less help, in fact, than in the USA. The feminist argument is that once all things are equal, it will be the norm for men to take parental leave at the same rate of women. But all things will never be equal. Far greater forces than utopian legislation and feminist zealotry are at work.

Forbes Magazine advises us that of the 1 011 billion-aires in 2010, a mere two per cent were women. The Center for Women's Business tells us that only 20% of the businesses earning over $1 million a year are owned by women. The World Economic Forum's *Global Gender Gap Report 2014*, meanwhile, indicated that it would take 81 years before women reached financial parity with men: if ever. And all this after four decades of the most inten-sive western investment in the promotion of women in the workplace, boardroom and in the registers of privately-owned businesses.

What are these reports flagging? The feminists ar-gue that the lack of equality in the work and business place is because of male resistance to change. They talk of glass ceilings. More interventions and more time will sort it all out, they assure us. The empiri-cal evidence, only a small part of it introduced in this Essay, is against it. Indeed, latest statistics indicate women are leaving work in greater numbers and earli-er than ever before. The turning point may have been reached.

And so we come to one of the great ironies of the Egalitarian Fantasy. The more the environmental excus-es are stripped away to explain the differences between individuals and groups, the more salient become immu-table genetic and biological factors. The more extremist feminists insist the genders are innately equal, the more they have to rely on intrusive and costly legislative and social interventions to achieve that elusive "equality" which we are assured is innate.

The obvious question is what is to be done. The answer: very little. The advent of women to the labour force is an accomplished fact and any attempt to reverse it would be disastrous for post-modern economies. It would in any case be absurd: not all women want to live according to traditional social roles. They have every right to pursue careers and search for the rewards that are obviously within reach.

Research by Queen's College in New York and augmented by further work by James Chung of Reach Advisors using US Census numbers, found in a 2014 report that unmarried, childless women under 30 years of age earned an average eight per cent more than their male peers in 147 out of the 150 major US cities surveyed.[24] Research by the Institute of Fiscal Studies in the UK, published in January 2015, revealed that while hourly wages for males in the UK during the recession had fallen 7.3%, it had dropped only 2.5% for women.

Such facts challenge the feminist argument that women are discriminated against *as women*. They earn less and are disadvantaged in terms of promotions because on average through a working lifetime they will work less and are less productive. The reasons for this, most obviously the critically important role traditionally played by women as home makers and care givers, are a different issue. The point is that where single women without encumbrances have made the tough choice between career and carer, they have equalled the pay of their comparable male counterparts and they have done so without expecting the society and the economy to fund them so they may pursue the benefits of both.

There is also no reason why we should not challenge the mindless and ideologically driven affirmative action projects demanding ever larger numbers of women in positions in the economy, academia, the public service and public office when we know its outcomes are not economically optimal, its effects put enormous strain on working mothers and, lastly, many women may not even want it. It is time for us to end, surely, these pointless exercises in national self-flagellation because women are not advancing in business/politics/academia at the rate the Franchise thinks they should. It is time to accept that the pace of that progress cannot be set by law-makers and social engineers but by other immutable and certain forces. Above all, surely it is time honestly and dispassionately to review the unintended consequences of this great social revolution.

No better example of the absurdity of this blind zeal for feminist equality can be found than in 2014 when the London Metropolitan Police admitted it could not reach its equality objectives amongst its firearms units because women did not feel comfortable with weapons or with the thought of killing people. The very next day the UK Ministry of Defence announced it was going to deploy women to serve in front-line positions. And a few months after that the MOD admitted that there were no more than 34 women who could be considered combat fit.

Amidst the greatest terrorist threat in recent history, growing Cyber attacks, asymmetrical wars across West and North Africa and the Middle East, the advent of Cold War II, the evolution of "hybrid war" in Eastern Europe, in the midst of all this, the deployment of 34 female soldiers engaged the minds of the military and large sections of the media. Such was the diverting power of the Egalitarian Fantasy.

Surely the most telling bit of research on the subject was the Advertising Age White Paper, The Rise of The Real Women, published in 2009. It showed that 36% of women professionals rated a career the "most important" thing in their life compared to 57% of males. Nearly sixty per cent of women put parenthood at the top of their list compared to 42% of males. The gap between male and female attitudes could not have been starker. The biological imperative was back big time [25]

IMMIGRATION AND THE EGALITARIAN FANTASY

The tale of unrestrained immigration of people from poorer parts of the world to the developed nations is a central part of the narrative of the Egalitarian Fantasy: and one of the most damaging in the modern era. The Fantasy naturally demanded a total equivalence between indigenous people and the newcomers. Thus was born the moral relativism and multiculturalism that triggered the slide-away from the core value system that had made Western democracies great and which had attracted immigrants in the first place.

In place of faith, family, work, loyalty, patriotism and discipline, the Left offered the Utopia of universal rights, universalism and the Egalitarian Fantasy. Although this appealed neither to the majority of indigenous western people nor to the immigrants, many of whom came from deeply conservative backgrounds, the triumph of the Leftist narrative was epically successful. The almost total control that the Left had wrested in academia, the media and western legal systems, saw to that.

Sixty years on, Western societies are battling to find values capable of being placed at the heart of their multi cultural societies. Indeed, in 2014, the Church of England was able to attack the Conservative Coalition for suggesting that "British Values" be placed at the heart of British education. This, they said, would be "divisive and undemocratic", thus posing the question of *whose* values they wanted to place at the heart of the nation's education or perhaps, more likely, they favoured no values at all. The immigrants had no such problem. They *knew* who they were and the values at the heart of their societies.

The biggest victims in all this have been the indigenous populations of the recipient nations because although the Fantasists insisted that immigrant groups could, should and in some cases *must* mobilise around their ethnicity and religion, the indigenous groups were ferociously attacked in law and by word if they attempted to do the same for themselves. In this melee, inevitably, new and insurgent beliefs, practices and values inserted themselves.

A significant body of research has now established that diverse societies or "culturally enriched" as the Left likes to call them, far from being a paradise of community harmony, are more fractured, distrustful and unsuccessful than homogenous ones.[1] Neither does mere wishful thinking by the disconnected elites about the universality of humankind ensure inter-racial harmony. Research in

the UK in 2014 uncovered the fact that despite six generations of incessant propagandizing by the elites, teenagers
were no more integrated with people from other racial
backgrounds than middle-aged ones, a telling reassertion
of the overriding biological imperative to muster with
one's own.[2].

The response of the Fantasists was of course not to
recognize this reality but to deny it. More measures to enforce integration were mooted. But by then the evidence
of material and deep-seated *differences* between communities was not only at hand but being debated openly in a
way that the traditional political elites were no longer able
to repress.

Indeed, the realisation that large numbers of immigrants from poor countries did not aspire to western values and in some cases actively sought to subvert
them, shocked the Western Liberal-Left into a catatonic
silence that has lasted for a decade. The Left has been unable to muster a single intelligent idea about how to deal
with the reality of deeply and sometimes violently con-
flicting values within their societies as a result of their
egalitarianism.

Particularly traumatic to the Left has been the implo-
sion of the belief that second generation immigrants will
inevitably adopt the values of their host countries. The

flow of home-born terrorists to the Middle Eastern wars exacerbated by western intervention, and the support they are given from their communities (as many as 27% of the young second-generation immigrant communities in the UK), the resurgence of fundamentalist beliefs, including religion, amongst a wide range of the immigrant young, gives the lie to the argument that time heals, that all immigrants just cannot wait to submerge themselves in the values of the host country.

Again, the reality that second generation UK Pakistani immigrants are more likely to engage in marriages by consanguinity, arranged via extended families still in their original tribal villages of origin, than the preceding one, has challenged the easy orthodoxy of the Left that immigrants would within a generation adopt the mores and customs of their host country rather than their country of origin.

The elitist response in times of crisis --- in the wake of the murder of a British soldier by Islamist extremists outside his barracks or the slaughter of civilians in the Paris massacres of early 2015 for example --- were always the same anaesthetic: mass "unity" rallies comprising all ethnic groups. These gatherings were therapeutic, laudable and even essential but it is absurd to suggest they could address the core issues: the reality of difference, the inability of the post-modern western state to protect its citizens from extremism and the increasing sense of alienation, anger and fear of the indigenous populations.

The mantra of the Western political elites following atrocities committed by extremists in the name of Muslims is also unchanged. Muslims as a group should not be held responsible for the actions of a few, they insist, while after every atrocity they rush to assure Muslims at large that there are no hard feelings.

Not surprisingly, this fails to gain much traction in a broad public which can point out with justification that although nobody could hold all Germans *responsible* for Nazi atrocities, they could be held *accountable* as a nation. Indeed for two generations, they were. All Japanese were held accountable for the excesses of the Bushido cult and indeed, to this day, the Left insists all Europeans and Americans be held accountable for slavery. Why should Muslims not be held accountable for the atrocious actions of their co-religionists, no matter what tiny minority they constitute or how deviant their views?

Muslims should not be punished or discriminated against; of course not. But it is fair to expect them to grasp that they, more than anybody else, have a duty to oppose and destroy the extremism that is perpetrating horror in their name. Muslim minorities in the developed world have been initially slow to pick up the challenge although, in fairness to them, they have hardly been under any pressure thus far from the western political leaders to do so.

It was precisely this sense of being unable to discuss the central reality of difference between people that so offended broad masses of the European public; the inability to frankly criticise the behaviour and attitudes of immigrant groups without being accused of either xenophobia or racism or having the dreaded knock at the door from what former British Prime Minister, Winston Churchill, so insightfully predicted in 1945 would be a policeman "very humanely directed in the first instance".

By 2013, merely by way of example, nearly all instances of electoral fraud in the UK were committed by Pakistani-descended UK citizens.[3] They had simply imported their "favour culture" into the ghetto's that had been created in their new homeland, courtesy of the Egalitarian Fantasy's multiculturalist aspirations.[4]

There were other problems. The fact that between 50 and 55 per cent of Pakistani marriages in the UK are between first cousins[5] and that an estimated 78% of Pakistani-descended people living in the UK are related by blood[6], raises an uncomfortable debate about the possible physical, emotional and mental impact on some of the community's young, and thus their vulnerability to the relentless indoctrination of extremist groups extolling Jihad.

Again, real tensions arose when second-generation children from achiever societies like China and India began to overtake the indigenous male white children from lower socio-economic groups at both school and work.[7] The immigrant children from failing societies, meanwhile, simply coalesced around the lowest level indigenous groups in their host countries, thus solidifying the very bottom layers of the social structure and making them even more intractable. This presented itself particularly in behaviour, social irresponsibility, poor parenting, music, dress and language.

Finally, perhaps most damning, in the UK town of Rochester, the sexual exploitation of young white girls from deprived areas by gangs disproportionately represented by people of Pakistani extraction, erupted into a national crisis in which accusations were made that state agencies had deliberately turned a blind eye to the exploitation for years out of a misplaced sense of multicultural tolerance.

Let us deal with the economics of immigration. A report by the Organisation for Economic Co-operation and Development in 2014, based on data collected over 50 years, found that immigration to developed world countries had been broadly fiscally neutral --- it had neither added to, nor subtracted from, benefit to their host countries.

Other research suggested that moderate immigration from countries of equivalent per capita GNP (other Western and some Central European nations, the former Dominions, Asia and North America) on balance created additional value to the host countries while rapid immigration from the rest on balance destroyed value.[8]

A joint University of London and University of California Los Angeles project in 2014, published in *The Economic Journal* in November 2014, came roughly to the same conclusion. The non-European Economic Area immigrants made a negative contribution to public finances in the UK of £591bn from 1995 to 2011. These 4.6m immigrants tended to be less skilled and have more children. In 2011, just under half were not working. Immigrants from within the European Economic Area, conversely, took out more than they put in for only seven of the 17 years reviewed. Their net contribution in the same period was £4.4bn positive.[9]

Paul Collier in his book, *Exodus* (2013) attempts to balance the debate: "Contrary to the prejudices of xenophobes, the evidence does not suggest that migration to date has had significant adverse effects on indigenous populations of host countries. Contrary to self-perceived "progressives", the evidence does suggest that without effective controls migration would rapidly accelerate to the point at which additional migration would have adverse effects, both on the indigenous populations of host societies and on those left behind in the poorest societies."[10]

The question remained. If there was no overall fiscal upside to host countries and possible negative downsides when immigrants from poor countries were admitted *end masse* to rich ones, why endure all the problems associated with mass immigration such as indigenous resistance, pressure on services and confusion of national identity? The answer: to serve the interests of the Egalitarian Fantasy and businesses wanting cheaper labour.

The Egalitarian Fantasy would of course brook no such vital distinction between value creators and value consumers, which is why the issue of immigration is now such a fierce point of political contestation in all developed world countries with its attendant risk of creating deep offence to the law-abiding, value-creating and loyal members of *all* the immigrant minorities.

Since the 1960's, a majority of British people have been against mass migration and by 2013 75% of British people wanted reduced migration according to opinion polls.[11] The fact that this widely-held belief was kept off the mainstream political agenda for so long, is testimony to the repressive powers of the

Western political elites and their supporting media. No longer, immigration now ranks amongst the foremost issues on the agendas of Western countries and right-of-centre parties have made huge electoral gains mobilizing around the issue, particularly in those southern European countries most on the front-line of illegal immigration.

A measure of the concern by the European elites about this groundswell of anger can be found in the surprising decision of the European Court of Justice in 2014 to uphold the rights of EU countries to deport economically unproductive immigrants. This court, which had done more than any other institution in the European Project to denigrate national sovereignty, attack the most sacrosanct traditions of member countries, abuse religious freedoms, undermine social cohesiveness and devalue the concept of fairness in the eyes of indigenous society, even this most monstrous and disconnected excrescence of the Egalitarian Fantasy, could feel the chill breeze of popular resent ment.

The ineffable tragedy is that a debate that could have been managed in a non-wounding way so much earlier if honestly addressed by the elites, has now spiralled into an ungenerous and often uninformed debate which fails to distinguish between the economic necessity and benefit of skilled immigration, on the one hand, with the mutually assured destruction of mass migration on the other. Everybody loses in the end.[12]

AND THE CULTURE

None of this can occur without great damage to the cultural life of nations or indeed humankind. The logical consequence of the Egalitarian Fantasy is twofold: nobody should hold excessive and ostentatious wealth and, second, no cultural artefact should be beyond the grasp of the lowest of the society.

Both conclusions have been faithfully and tragically implemented. The great wealth that throughout our recent history has been devoted by individuals, institutions, monarchies and the religious authorities to the creation of enduring beauty --- architecture, music, art --- is now limited.. Not since the 19th Century have wealthy people or institutions dared to devote their wealth and prestige to something as ephemeral and elitist as the creation of beauty for its own sake.

Had the Egalitarian Fantasy existed throughout history we would have no great capitals of the world, no extraordinary examples of architecture, no alluring galleries, no breath-taking concerts; just thousands of square miles of modest abodes resounding every night to the sounds of Little Britain, Strictly Come Dancing, the X Factor or Rap music.

A great divide has opened, a black hole, which historians of the Western civilizations in the distant future will regard with incomprehension. They will find plenty of examples of rich people acquiring already created beauty during the reign of The Egalitarian Fantasy, often for no other reason than the boasting of it. They will find the wealthy American foundations to be generous patrons of the arts. They will find abundant evidence of large numbers of people who support created beauty in many of its forms. They will wonder at the millions of humans who flocked to concerts of aging rock stars merely to recreate a nostalgic moment of past virtuosity. But how many will be the patrons in the creation of enduring beauty. The answer is few and for a simple reason.

The Egalitarian Fantasy insists that contemporary realised Art be no more than within the grasp of the lowest orders of intelligence and sensibility. To do otherwise would betray the Fantasy. Who would want to support the mediocrity of such ambition? And thus, sadly, the prodigious investment of the developed world into modern creativity will do no more than assuage an immediate appetite for titillation. It will create nothing of endurance. It will be a fleck of dust on the surface of a Michelangelo fresco or a Bernini sculpture or the score sheet for a

Mozart masterpiece, a black hole in the centuries-long cultural history of the Western empires, surely the direst consequence of The Egalitarian Fantasy.

Harold Bloom in his masterful *The Western Canon,* written in 1994[1], addresses this tension between the aesthetics at the heart of Western literature and the attacks on it by the Left, the Marxists, Feminists and Historicists who seek to reduce art to nothing but the interplay of historical and economic forces. By so doing, of course, they reduce all art to nothing but an artefact of political process. And here a great irony: the same people who would pillory Renaissance art as being no more than a propaganda device for Christianity, who vilify Caravaggio as the poster maker of post-Reformation Catholicism, who attack the Dutch Masters as being the image makers of the wealthy, who brand the greatest writers of Western literature as no more than the mouthpieces of bourgeois economic interests, these same people are quite happy to suborn art to the imperatives of modern class and ideological warfare.

The result is inevitable: art and literature becomes revered not for what it means to people as *art* but becomes judged on whether it advances this or that cause. The artist who collects the commissions does so not for his or her skill but for correctness. As we know, the causes advanced by the Egalitarian Fantasy have all been based on a false premise and so too their diminution of what Bloom calls the Western Canon: as in everything, they turn gold dust to bull dust. The premises are tumbling but the damage has been done.

Bloom calls these attackers of the Western Canon the School of Resentment and observes of their relentless assault on the Bard: "Originality is the great scandal that resentment cannot accommodate"[2]

He is correct in his identification of the battle lines but fails at the last hurdle. *Why* do certain individuals display extraordinary virtuosity in specific forms of art or why are national groups associated with excellence in particular art forms ? Why is it possible to have an informed discussion about Caravaggio with a clothing store attendant in Valletta when the average equivalent in, say, America, would think one was asking about a pizza? Why can a group of *Carabinieri* doing escort duty for a dignitary in Rome break into a magnificent aria of a popular opera on request? Why, when one attends a Church service anywhere in Africa, can one be swept away instantly by the effortless, untutored melodiousness of the congregation as it rises to song? Why are the Jewish people such huge contributors to the pantheon of the world's greatest classical musicians and creators of music in all its forms? Or the Russians the foremost exponents of dance? And why do the English and French-speaking worlds still retain dominance in the multiplicity and virtuosity of the written word ? Economics and history cannot account for all of it. Culture alone does not. It is deeper. It must be as much in the genes and the biology. And it is heritable.

POLITICAL EFFECTS

The growing gap between the top and lower ends of society was manageable while the developed world was able to dispense sufficient money, at first through earnings and then through debt. The winners simply bought off the losers. But when the system had been brought to crisis through the Egalitarian Fantasy and when the money had run out, the differences between the have and have-not groups, nations, races and classes became brutally exposed.

This tension underlies all of current political contestation in the developed world, as indeed it has through history. The fight, a bare-knuckled one, is now between the conservative wealth-holding and wealth-creating groups on the one hand, and the wealth-consuming ones on the other, with a large and destabilising injection of nihilism from a new class of cynical, embittered and suspicious activists, products of the general collapse of faith wrought by a demonstrably failed Egalitarian Fantasy.

The immediate cause of this is something ridiculously simple. Take away all the theorising, mountains of books, solemn pronunciations, endless conferences, newspaper columns and blogs, battalions of talking heads on TV, take this all away and at the heart of the current crisis-faced Western modernity is the collapse of the oldest value of civilised order: the concept of reciprocity.

This principle determines that if I do something for you, you do something back for me. It need not be a precisely equivalent exchange, indeed it would be pointless if it were, but both parties have at least to feel there is something in it for them. This has been the basis of social organization through all history. The hunting party leader shares food and his underlings surrender first call on the prime females and rally to support the leader if another band attacks. The medieval monarch allocates land and privilege to his barons; they provide money and men to defend the realm. The landed barons provide employment and tenancies; the peasants render labour and soldiering and respect. Finally, we surrender a whole range of rights and resources to the modern state and its laws; that state reciprocates by providing services, stability, equality before the law, sound currencies and security. Where this reciprocity becomes asymmetrical, where one side unjustifiably demands more from the other or one party is unable, or refuses, to deliver its part, this precarious contract is broken.

Then societies shiver and often sunder. It is happening now.

The Egalitarian Fantasy blew this reciprocity to bits. From the perspective of the wealth creating sector, they continued to surrender wealth and resources to the state in a spiralling quantum, while the wealth consumers did the reverse. Their tax burden declined. State taxation systems penalized the savers and subsidised the spenders. Whereas once the rich could get away with working shorter but smarter hours than the less skilled, now the lower skilled were working less --- eight hours a week less --- and many were not working at all.[1] In short, seen from the wealth creators' perspective, the poor did less, offered less, demanded more and maintained a constant stream of vituperation against the rich and the financial institutions that were the source of everyone's wealth.

As the institutions, primarily those of law but also the social and developmental agencies, turned increasingly to defend the interests of the wealth-consumers against the wealth-creators, the element of reciprocity finally soured. With it went trust, the very basis of contract, law, institutions and social cohesiveness.

And so, in response to a pervasive egalitarianism that offered them no advantage, the wealth creators increasingly withdrew from any sense of social reciprocity and because they were bright and knowledgeable and had control of the levers of real power, they were effective and dangerous. Enter buccaneering capitalism, exploitation of consumers, tax evasion, avoidance and outright fraud. An unaccountable global meritocracy replaced a localised, accountable business elite. Captain Mainwaring was usurped by the Wolf of Wall Street. The response was inevitable: more hatred for the wealth creating classes, more populist revolt and more clueless and self-serving intervention by the political elites.

The immediate background to this struggle was the collapse of the Soviet Union in the late 1980's. This most extreme form of the Egalitarian Fantasy failed through the weight of its own implausibility, yet the causes of that collapse were uncomfortably similar to the ones which created the later crisis of the developed world --- economies no longer able to generate the wealth needed to sustain their own expensive mythologies.

So when Francis Fukuyama wrote his iconic *The End of History and the Last Man*, which proclaimed the decisive victory of the idea of the liberal market economy over communism[2], he was only partly correct. He had not counted on the effects of the Egalitarian Fantasy. Instead of appreciating that the collapse of communism must logically be followed by the destruction of *all* socialist, welfarist and redistributive systems, the leaders of the

West chose to see it as the end only of the *Soviet* form of egalitarianism.

He also failed to anticipate a far more important development which a colleague, Sam Huntington, did in his book *Culture Clash: The Remaking of the World Order,* written in the same year. Huntington identified the end of the battle of ideology as presaging a new contest: that of culture. In the short term it has manifested itself in the rise of militant Islamism. In the long-term it will be the contest between wealth-creators and wealth-consumers in the developed world, a tension overlaid with generational, racial, regional, cultural and genetic overtones.

Both conflicts have the same cause: the Egalitarian Fantasy. In the former case the Fantasy let Islamic extremism root in developed world countries thanks to multiculturalism and a hopelessly naïve sense of "tolerance". The Egalitarian Fantasy also drove western governments to intervene in deeply divided foreign countries, with catastrophic consequences. In the looming battle between wealth creators and wealth consumers, the Fantasy gutted the lower socio-economic orders in economic, political and social terms, attacked the wealth creators and ceded economic competitiveness to others.

Western forms of egalitarianism, the Egalitarian Fantasy, powered ahead without restraint. Indeed, it became even more extreme and because of that was obliged to rest its fortunes to an ever greater extent on robustly growing economies. Thus the Faustian Pact between the Egalitarian Fantasy and the worst and most egregious forms of capitalism in our history. The deal from the side of populist governments was simple: *you* make the taxes to pay for the Egalitarian Fantasy any way you think fit and *we* will spend it any way *we* think fit.

As we now know, this was a fatal error and the quality of political leadership that could have moderated this pact, a Reagan or a Thatcher, was no longer around. The developed world's political and financial models outlasted the Soviet model by a scant quarter of century before they too were on the ropes, eviscerated by the Egalitarian Fantasy.

This tension between the have's and the have-nots, underlies the most recent UK, US, French and Italian elections. It has been greatly exacerbated in Europe by the crisis of the single currency, itself an extreme ideological expression of the Egalitarian Fantasy, the belief that simply because nations share a common geographical area they are equal and will behave the same.[3]

It is a finely balanced contest. A coffee shop analysis of the last eight major developed world elections would suggest the parties that claim the support of the wealth creating classes draw about 30% of the electorate. The bottom of the scale classes constitute about 20% of the electorate and vote for redistributive parties, when they bother to vote at all.

The remaining 50% are balanced between those who fall into what could be called the marginally value adding classes, currently about 20% of the total, and the marginally value detracting ones, about 30%. This brings us back to the roughly half of developed world country households who add economic value versus the half which detract value.

It is for the support of this 50% floating vote along a fluctuating notional value line, this so-called squeezed middle class, that nearly all political contestation now takes place.[4] It is also the range most susceptible to indigenous political impulse: the Greek Syrizia socialists, the Italian Five Star movement, the French Front National, the United Kingdom Independence Party.[5]

It is because the issues are so stark and the margins so narrow, that the tenor of the political debate has become sharp and vituperative. This culminates a long process during which the protagonists of the Egalitarian Fantasy on the left upped their violent defence of the status quo, even as its failure became ever more apparent.

And this highly tensile politics is being played out in a radically changed environment.

First, the loss of faith in politics and indeed institutions brought about by financial collapse and the inversion of core values by the Egalitarian Fantasy, has turned large numbers of voters, particularly the young, away from the main stream parties which they hold to be responsible for the crisis, or at the very least the confusion.

In its place has come the advent of the special interest group, enormously empowered by the mobilizing force of social media. These groups, subjecting all issues of national-al interest to the narrow prism of their randomly selected special cause, have shattered the capacity of the traditional political classes to define the central issues, control the debate and build coherent alliances around them. As the single issue groups are usually the most vociferous and passionate, they are also likely to be the most extremist.

Inevitably, the modern state has moved towards ad hoc management of a running series of disconnected issues, each one won or lost to the extent to which the special in-terests can mobilise overwhelming force on the ether via Twitter deluge or on the street via Facebook flashmob or other social media agitprop. An essential lubricant for this process has to be hyperbole --- why else would anybody pay attention amid all the other noise. And this in turn has given rise to the defining feature of modern developed world political discourse, indiscriminate hysteria.

Few issues, let alone something as challenging as debating the Egalitarian Fantasy, can be addressed with caution, detachment and rationality. This plays directly to the interests of the Egalitarian Fantasy and the powerful mandarins of the disaggregated state which in this *fin de siècle,* regard reasoned debate as a mortal threat. This may be pure, anarchic democracy. But it is an impossible way in which to manage complex modern states.

Bizarrely, the leaders of developed countries seemed quite happy to throw their weight behind these inorganic demonstrations of protest when they occurred elsewhere, apparently pleased to see established and recognized governments toppled left, right and centre in the developing world through nothing more than the force of Facebook crowds.

These mobs, beloved of the developed world elites because they appeared so much like *us,* were in every case rapidly swept from the streets and from history by the hard men with the real power. And then the blood flowed, at which point the West, like Scott Fitzgerald's Tom and Daisy Buchanan in *The Great Gatsby*, retreated into the vast indifference of their wealth. Little did the Western political elites realize that it may be their turn next, so fragile is the remaining consensus in developed world polities.

This brings us to the second change in the political environment --- a collapsed locus of power in the modern Western state. Thanks to The Egalitarian Fantasy, huge tracts of power once held by accountable, central governments has been ceded to outliers. One thinks immediately of the European Union, unions, oversight bodies, multinational agencies, international courts of human rights, single issue lobbies, charities and so endlessly on.

Many of these institutions were created to advance the Egalitarian Fantasy. Others were created just to make work. All, without exception, ended up advancing the interests of "progressive" and Leftist forces. They now constitute a terrifying layer of powerful, unelected, unaccountable mandarins headed for the most part by ideological extremists. Most of them are from the Left and for a simple reason. When conservative and traditionalist politicians lose office they tend to return to what they were doing before, which is usually in business or the professions. When Left wing politicians lose power, they tend to search around for another source of public succour, which is why they are so disproportionately represented in these unaccountable agencies. More darkly, one may suggest they are deliberately placed leftist moles, the classic "entryist" cadres.

In an attempt to support a process which was ostensibly to make democracy broader and more accountable, conservative political forces acquiesced in the destruction of the power of the central state to implement the mandates of elected conservative and traditionalist parties. This impotence of governments, particularly ones with a traditionalist or conservative orientation, is fuelling the growing public impatience with established politics. Why bother electing a government when it has no real power? Why put one's faith in a new government to change anything when they cannot? Why bother to defend democracy at all?

The net effect of this cynicism has been a catastrophic drop in the number of people belonging to political parties or bothering to turn out to elections. It also places the established parties in a quandary. They know that to return developed world governments to effectiveness and credibility they have to take back power for the State. But to do so would open them up to charges of authoritarianism. So here is yet another irony. To advance the interests of the egalitarian project they have destroyed their own power and credibility.

The consequence of this castration of central government power was seen across the UK and Europe in 2014 when new right wing challenger parties in northern Europe and left wing ones in southern Europe, exploded onto the political scene in hitherto unimaginable force. The message was clear: the neglected indigenous conservative forces of Western democracies had found their voice again, this time outside the mainstream parties. They were pushing back against the sense of powerlessness in the face of the disconnectedness, arrogance and misdirection of the political elites.

The third critical change in the political environment is the fact that the gap between governed and governing classes in the developed world is now wider than ever in recent modern history. The annual British Social Attitudes Survey of 2014 was constrained to observe a widening disconnect between the "liberal political classes" and public opinion --- much of it focused on the vexed question of immigration and the broader question of the meaning of British identity.

The same could be said of every other developed world country. After decades of The Egalitarian Fantasy, broad public opinion had finally awoken to the fact that it was, and is, one of the greatest misadventures of history. By refusing honestly to acknowledge difference between individuals and communities, by denying the existence of unequal capabilities in individuals and groups, by neglecting to respect those differences and, finally, by failing to manage difference sensitively, intelligently and proportionately, the Egalitarian Fantasy has left a baleful inheritance.

Again, let us count the ways:

- The western political elites promised an end to "boom and bust" economies. They presided over the most egregious forms of capitalist endeavour in history and delivered the worst financial melt down in 60 years, a moment that brought Western financial systems to the brink of collapse. All of this was to fund the massive social welfare costs they had incurred, were incurring and would incur in the future.
- They assured that huge state investments in lower socio-economic groups would result in them rising majestically to opportunity. A reduction in inequality would follow. In reality, income gaps widened to unprecedented levels and the lowest quintile spun off into the direst dependency and social pathology.
- They pledged cradle to grave welfare. Instead, in many cases, they bequeathed broken health, educational and pension schemes. Without even the courage to admit the failings, they busied themselves with tinkering at the edges. Those countries still providing high level services in health and education are doing so at an astronomical and unsustainable cost. Await the crash.
- They destroyed old and core values of nations, replacing them instead with febrile concepts of

internationalism, globalism, an exotic spread of human rights and the promise of an ill-defined equality, divorced from biological and genetic reality. None of this had traction or resonance amongst the broad community. How little traction is now being noticed as it plays out in polling stations in many advanced Western democracies.

- They promised that mass immigration would enrich developed world societies. It did not, at least not sufficiently, and certainly not to its promise. It created tensions and anger amongst indigenous populations and profound disillusionment amongst poor immigrants.

- The liberal left guaranteed that multiculturalism would ensure harmony and social cohesiveness. Not a chance. It allowed certain immigrant groups to embed themselves and their alien cultures in their new homes, free to espouse values sometimes in direct conflict with those of their hosts. The indigenous population, meanwhile, was intimidated into disowning -- at least on the surface and in public -- its own heritage, culture and values to the cause of multiculturalism.

- They promised that across the developing world, repressed societies were just waiting to be liberated by the force of armed Western moral imperialism to become model democracies. The ashes of that myth lie before us in Iraq, Yemen, Egypt, Libya, the Sahel, Syria, Northern Nigeria and soon, again, Afghanistan.

- In the case of Europe, this leadership promised economic advancement and unity through a federalised Europe. They have brought decades of economic stagnation, unemployment, rising nationalism and most latterly, a bitter civil war on the periphery because of their expansionist pretensions.

- In every field of human endeavour "experts" preached on, warned about, threatened, explicated on and denounced everything from levels of human salt intake to Full English Breakfasts. Eighty per cent of what they published and which was breathlessly reported by the popular media, was subsequently withdrawn, never validated or found to be dead wrong.

- The "experts" assured the world that it was on a path to perdition with ever rising temperatures as a result of anthropogenic carbon emissions. Seventeen years on the world's temperature had hardly moved but massive "green" imposts have critically weakened Western competitiveness, endangered energy security and laid heavy cost burdens on the poorest of the world's populations.

- Finally, these elites, had promised to lead the developed world in its unbroken march towards improved lifestyles, education, health and morality. The reverse is true. For the first time in Western history, outside cataclysmic war, today's young people face declining incomes, reduced job opportunities, diminished educational standards, lower standards of mass health, slowing social migration and wide-scale confusion about identity and core morality.

On every point, then, on every point, the Left and liberal political elites have been wrong. They have epically misled the developed world. And now they reap the harvest in a bitterly angry or contemptuous polity, ripe for change. The risk, an enormous one, is that this revulsion with the elites will lead to extremist authoritarian options --- left or right.

Let us be clear where the heart of this revolt lies. It is not just a right-wing rebellion against the left or a left-wing rebellion against the centre, as in Greece. It is not a protest vote by disillusioned conservatives against historic party machines. It is not a straight fight between poor and rich. It is not xenophobia. It is not a continuation of the tiresomely familiar squabble between the decaying 20th century mainstream party political systems in a different guise.

It is, rather, an upwelling of anger by the developed world's value creators and defenders at all levels of the society against the value consumers and destroyers and those who purport to represent them. It is a reassertion of the oldest values by which western nations have organised themselves, that of faith, family, culture, patriotism and work. And, crucially, it is a reassertion of common sense by ordinary people from all strata of society against the manifest disconnection of the elites from the realities of life and human nature.

In every failure of the Western elites world view can be counted the same achingly familiar theme: a refusal to grant the importance of genetic and biological difference in the formation of individuals and the social, political and economic structures to which they give life.

Intriguingly, research by evolutionary geneticists increasingly suggests that the economic status of voters in Western countries is by no means the most important determiner of voting preference. Poor people vote for conservative parties in about the same proportion as wealthy people vote for liberal parties. The reason they do so lies in something much more profound than Marxist views about false consciousness. It literally lies in their biological wiring, a network laid down eons ago and it divides those with a predisposition to support economic and social dominant groups, to be part of those groups, versus those with a predisposition to identify with subordinate groups --- the underdogs.[6]

But such discoveries are of course anathema to the Left. They belie simplistic propositions that human attitudes are a direct and inevitable consequence of social formations. The discoveries imply that what counts in this world is what people *are,* not what society can potentially *make* of them. Such an argument of course denies any meaningful role for social interlocutors in making people winners. It refutes the Egalitarian Fantasy. It challenges millions of non-jobs and pensions.

It is because of this that the vociferous camps in defence of the Egalitarian Fantasy have come to the fore in wide alliance: the political left, the bureaucracies, the educational establishments, the liberal-left legal establishment, unions, churches and charities. The one thing joining them all (apart from a shared lexicon of despairingly vacuous cliché) is an unswerving determination to keep as many free born citizens as possible in a state of dependence, servitude, insecurity, fear and incapacity. The livelihood of this alliance depends on it.

Mortal foes to this grand alliance are the qualities of independent thinking, enthusiasm, optimism, self-reliance and self-sufficiency, the very attributes the genetic sciences tells us are to a considerable extent embedded in humans, not inculcated. If people are not born to be unfree, they have to be forced to be unfree, insists the Egalitarian Fantasy. .

A core strategy in this process of "unfreeing" developed world populations has been the expansion of law. In the tenure of Prime Minister Tony Blair in the UK, for example, 26 000 new laws were passed, many intruding into arenas of life which had up till then been regulated perfectly satisfactorily between individuals. What had once been considered misfortune or absent-mindedness or insensitivity or just bad manners, suddenly became actionable tort and subject to extreme penalties.[7]

In so doing the socialists in Britain were of course doing no more than building on the tradition left by their forefathers in 1945 when they came to power and simply re-purposed the whole intrusive and omnipresent regulatory regime of Britain-at-total-war into serving the interests of the socialist state and its later derivatives, the welfare and nanny states.

British Prime Minister Winston Churchill warned at the time of a "new Gestapo" in the event of a socialist win.[8] It is worth recalling those famous words in their entirety: *"No Socialist Government conducting the entire life........ of the country could afford to allow free, sharp or violently-worded expressions of public discontent. They would have to fall back on some form of Gestapo, no doubt very humanely directed in the first instance. And this would nip opinion in the bud: it would stop criticism as it reared its head, and it would gather all the power to the supreme party and the party leaders, rising like stately pinnacles above their vast bureaucracies of Civil Servants, no longer servants and no longer civil."*

He lost the 1945 elections but was proved right. The new Gestapo can be found throughout the developed world with unparalleled powers of interference in the lives of ordinary citizens, surveillance and repression of free expression. In the UK, for example, more than 20 different authorities have the power of unconstrained egress to the homes of citizens. Very few citizens in the UK can walk to the corner shop to buy milk without being tracked by CCTV camera, smartphones and internet activity.

Critical areas of human life are determined by extraordinary powers and secret courts such as the UK's Court of Protection. In a landmark judgment in 2013, Sir James Munby, President of the UK's High Court Family Division, flagged the concerns of a number of judges about the way social services were wresting children away from their parents and putting them up for adoption. In his judgment, Munby ordered that removal from the care of biological parents should be an extreme and last resort and that all other avenues be explored first, such as placing the children with relatives.

The result of the judgment was to see a 47% fall in the number of children put forward for adoption. There was no evidence that this had resulted in any increased instance of children being put at risk. By any definition possible, a fall in the number of children being put up for adoption would be counted as a victory, a triumph for sensible and sensitive management of fractured families, an affirmation of a healthy social environment. No chance. The National Adoption Leadership Board, charged with overseeing the reforms, described it as "alarming". And the popular media branded it, of course, a "crisis". Supercrisis.org could smell a threat to its business model a mile off.

The UK's Court of Protection, meanwhile, notoriously ordered in 2013 that the unborn baby of an Italian woman be delivered by caesarean section and immediately put up for adoption, despite the fact that the Judge accepted the woman was well, taking her medication and had a job. The father and in-laws had also offered to care for the child. The order, demanded by the welfare services, was granted after a secret hearing from which the family were excluded.[9]

It is easy to see how such a thing could happen. The promise of the Egalitarian Fantasy to its public is not just about equality and the good life but also about a total *lack of risk,* all to be achieved by legal and administrative fiat. It is a chimera of course but in its pursuit modern states, individually or as collectives, have assumed ever more draconian powers to regulate social issues in their futile efforts to deliver the unattainable.

Worse, in the belief that the world is risk free, it is obvious that where risk occurs and results in damage or fatality, somebody must be to blame. The question is who. It cannot be God since the Egalitarian Fantasy has destroyed God. It cannot be the Egalitarian Fantasy itself. That would destroy it. It must either be externalities, in which case we are all guiltless, or it is individuals, in which case they must be hunted and exposed. And so we have the relentless pursuit of individuals or organisations to be denounced to the mobs as responsible, often for the most basic of human errors or honest misjudgement. And so again, the Egalitarian Fantasy delivers not its promise of justice and fairness but the very opposite: witch hunts and scapegoating. Yet again, it delivers not a brave new world, but a Medieval one.

And of course, huge swathes of the society, decent, honest people, are seduced into the belief that it is all in a good cause. Easily then, do they snap into the snitch mode and, Stasi-style, they inform on their neighbours in vast, disconcerting numbers. Such denunciations bring only further insecurity. At its logical and inevitable conclusion, its final Egalitarian absurdity, babies are ripped from mother's wombs against their wishes or that of their families, elderly people showing evidence of forgetfulness are forcibly separated from their children because they have "dementia", pet cats are put to death because their owners fail to groom them adequately, a 43-year-old mother of three disabled children smothers them and then attempts to commit suicide because she can no longer endure the

intrusive behaviour of the 60 health care professionals in-
terfering in her household, good people making innocent
errors are hauled before the Inquisition, entire football
teams arrested for rape on the say-so of one disturbed
woman, 1 400 young girls fall into prostitution rings run
predominantly by men of foreign extraction during a 16
year period in Rotherham so as not to undermine the multicultural mythology, a young man is denied custody of his
child because in his youth he belonged to a right-wing political movement of which the social service officer disap-
proved, a 63-year-old women is hauled from her bed and
spends two days in the police cells because she "biffed"
her husband with a newspaper in a row over which TV
channel to watch and a 17-year-old girl is taken to the cells
for a similar row with her younger sister, policemen surge
onto football terraces to seize people they think may have
been making "racially offensive gestures" or prosecute
Twitter users who jokingly threaten to 'bomb' an airport
if the weather fails to improve. These incidents are not
hyperbole; they are not part of some Kafkaesque drama.
They are part of the recent record of courts in the UK.[10]

Thus are the prohibitions on "hate speech" invoked
with an increasing and oppressive regularity to avert dis-
cussions about the false premises of the egalitarian project; the police actions against "hate" speech or its feminist
equivalent, "sexual harassment" or "domestic violence",
become ever more pointless, random and vindictive; with

Pavlovian predictability, politicians call for inquiries and witch hunts into vast organisations on the mere whiff of suspicion of moral deviance at some distant past date --- paedophilia, precisely because of its indisputable insult to public mores, is a classic and easily mobilized trigger point. In pursuit of the Egalitarian Fantasy, swathes of public life and debate in the developed world are at risk of falling subject to arbitrary, repressive and unaccountable authority to a degree arguably unmatched since the inquisitorial Middle Ages.

This crucial change in the nature of human organisation has been explained by a French philosopher as a shift from structure of "discipline" to one of "control".[11] It works this way: in earlier social forms, humans were ordered into hierarchical systems of discipline within clearly understood parameters, whether family, school, barracks, university or factory floor. People not only understood their individual relationship with power but the expectations that went with it. Whether they accepted that relationship or thought it fair was irrelevant. They understood it. There was a context to it.

This has been destroyed --- I would argue by the Egalitarian Fantasy --- and in its place has come the notion of total control. This control is partly exercised through massively intrusive administrative law which for the most part is not explicit --- how can it be explicit when actions committed forty years ago are suddenly judged in terms of a maliciously manufactured contemporary exigency. How can it be explicit when what once was just inconsiderate or boorish behaviour is suddenly post-facto converted to a crime – in the most egregious cases to Orwellian "hate speech crime"-- and subject to criminal sanction.

This new social control has no clear parameters and no discernible hierarchy. It does not even have a clearly stated objective or outcome. It comes through marketing manipulation, social media, intrusive state interference through unaccountable regulatory bodies and NGO's and the calculated creation by vested interests of periodic states of national hysteria to achieve short-term political or financial ends. The ghost of ancient superstition stalks us all today, thanks to these forces.

Anybody who doubts this, needs to consider the implications of the revelation in 2014 that Facebook had conducted a massive research project on its subscribers without their knowledge or consent to test their emotional response to deprivation --- in this case they were sent false messages telling them they had been unsubscribed. How is that for unaccountable control?

The developed world teeters thus perilously close to slipping into a new totalitarianism in defence of a scientific myth, not for the first time in history.

THE BROADER IMPLICATIONS

The rising powers of the world are not sitting still in the face of the baleful consequences of the developed world's indulgence of the Egalitarian Fantasy. In 2012, for the first time, south-south trade exceeded north-south trade and for the first time foreign direct investment (FDI) into developing countries outstripped that into developed countries. The four most important of these emerging economies, Brazil, Russia, India and China, were responsible for 55% of global economic growth between 2009 and 2012, China being the major contributor. The 23 countries of the developed world, by comparison, contributed 20%, mostly from Germany and the US. The picture changed slightly thereafter as the Euro Zone countries slid further into depression, the UK and the USA showed resurgent growth and Brazil and Russia experienced sharp slow-downs in growth --- the latter a consequence of falling oil prices and Western sanctions after the Ukrainian crisis of 2014-15.[1]

By 2013, GDP for the EU and US totalled $34.2 tr while GDP from the BRIC countries (Brazil, Russia. India and China) totalled $29.6 tr. The continuing anaemic performance of the Eurozone and the US slow-down meant that tip-over point was fast approaching. China finally pipped the US to first place as the largest economy in the world in 2014 measured by certain criteria.

But more to the point, currency reserves, the very basis of the US's continued domination of world finance and trade, was under threat, as was dollar dominance sustained by its petro-dollar position. The BRIC countries accounted for half of global currency reserves and the developing world as a totality more than three quarters. More scarily, the G7 nations controlled less than 20% and if one excludes Japan, it was eight per cent.

Nothing is written in stone and this may well change. Developing countries still have to confront the huge challenges of managing exuberant social expectations, inflamed by social media demagoguery, with a slow down in their traditional markets. In many of these developing nations the mix of export and internal production is skew or, in the case of Russia, they are too dependent on resources. In others, business cultures and institutions have not caught up with rampant economic growth; they remain trapped in age-old habits of corruption, sloth and nepotism. The US, meanwhile, may still surprise with the extent of its recovery on the back of its decisive consolidation and the short term bonanza of cheap gas and oil. But the reality, the general reality, is that the *potential* for material long term growth lies no longer in the aged economies but in the new ones.

These powerful new emergent market entities are seeking to confront and challenge the old orthodoxies: the World Trade Organisation treaties and the Bretton Woods institutions. In 2014, the BRIC countries announced the formation of the New Development Bank with capitalization of £50bn, similar to the World Bank, and the Contingent Reserve Arrangement with $100bn currency reserve, counterpart to the International Monetary Fund, now seriously compromised by its efforts to save the failed politically-inspired single currency of Europe. These arrangements seek to cushion BRIC countries from volatilities caused by the developed world economies. There is even a military threat, most obviously from Russia.

All of these challenges arise directly from the Egalitarian Fantasy's weakening of the systems and structures created by the developed world after the last World War to ensure that "never again" would such destruction be waged. The global financial systems set up so optimistically to prevent a repetition of the Great Depression are now bled white by the efforts to resuscitate developed world economies after the fall-out of 2008, the rolling liquidity, sovereign debt and banking crises generated by the economic illiteracy of a single, egalitarian European currency for vastly different economies.[2]

The organization set up to defend Europe against Soviet expansionism, the North Atlantic Treaty organization, is now in a profound crisis of identity. Lulled by the collapse of the Soviet Union, the military alliance which more than anything else enabled the West to outlive the implausibility of the Soviet's own Egalitarian Fantasy, chose to wind down its capacity, just as others were building theirs and as new threats were looming.

The major NATO powers allowed themselves to be drawn into endless wars in Middle Eastern and North African countries, not as purely defensive military endeavours but as political and social ones. The objective of destroying the Taliban in Afghanistan was winnable and was indeed achieved in the months immediately after 9/11. Then the Egalitarian Fantasy intervened. The objective became the creation of a stable and peaceful modern democracy in Afghanistan; to stop the harvesting of poppies and the return of 14-year-old girl children to school. That battle, utterly noble, as anybody who knew either history or biology, was an unwinnable one, at least in anything but the very long term --- and modern popular democracies do not do long term. It has been reduced, I gravely suspect, to the attention span of a Twitter message.

The capacity to maintain this level of defence expenditure by the West was in any case flagging; the major parties were becoming tetchy with each other. All NATO countries had pledged to invest two per cent of GDP in defence. Only France and Britain complied, and even then the latter under its Conservative Coalition cut defence spending at precisely the point it committed itself to ever greater global efforts to project its moral imperialism and egalitarianism. Why this under-investment in defence? The resources were being diverted elsewhere: to fund the Egalitarian Fantasy at home.

The United States, meanwhile, had other things on its mind. Like China. In 1962, 277 000 US forces were based in Europe. By 2014, 85% had been withdrawn and senior US officials were warning Europe it must take responsibility for its future defence. It was this fatal gap between Western pretensions of power and Western capacity and willingness to deploy power that Russia's Vladimir Putin read so perfectly, first in Georgia and then the Ukraine.

The 2013 Ukrainian crisis was indeed a case study. The West, particularly the EU, endorsed the overthrow of a pro-Russian, constitutionally elected head-of-state, Viktor Yanukovych, through threat of extremist violence, in direct contravention of a peace deal brokered by the EU itself, a deal in which the besieged President had conceded to *all* the demands of the protestors. The action had been preceded by months of Facebook-facilitated street protests which had paralysed the country's capital and led to a calibrated escalation of provocation by the protestors against state authority, every step supported by the EU.

The overthrow of an elected European leader by the mobs and subsequent threats of discriminatory measures against ethnic Russian Ukrainians by the putchists, gave the perfect opportunity for the intervention of Putin, a revanchist nationalist, who argued that his effective annexation of Crimea and parts of eastern Ukraine was necessary to protect ethnic Russians.

The Ukrainian Government's response was to deploy military forces to repress the rebels in the East, thus prompting a bloodbath which exceeded by a factor of hundreds the number of people killed in the original protests in Kiev. It is difficult to know what else Kiev could do to suppress a violent insurrection on its sovereign territory, but that is not the point. The crisis could have been de-escalated if the Ukrainian parties had kept to the EU-brokered deal and if they had given Russia the guarantee they wanted that they would not join NATO.

After all, if plucky Finland managed to keep good relations with the Russian Bear for half a century with a far more forbidding lot in the Kremlin, why could Ukraine not have done the same? It was dissuaded from doing so by the European Union's fantasy that moral imperialism will triumph; that countries can ignore the reality of their geographical location, their history and their culture in pursuit of noble egalitarian outcomes.

It all ended in tears. It always does. If the Ukraine had counted on Western military support to oppose Russian intervention, it was to be disappointed. Where Putin put 140 000 troops into an exercise along his borders with Ukraine, annexed Crimea by stealth and sponsored a military *cordon sanitaire* in Eastern Ukraine, NATO responded by Steadfast Jazz 2013 in Poland, the largest live-fire exercise since 2006. Six thousand NATO troops were involved. The West turned instead to the blunt, imperfect and often boomeranging instrument of economic sanctions. Putin simply faced them down; confident of domestic support and the view that the West would never challenge him militarily.

The lesson in this rather extended diversion into Eastern European politics? The crisis could have been avoided had the Egalitarian Fantasists of the EU not, on the basis of Facebook emotionalism, sought to impose their views on a country riven with deep and historical divides.. What was needed was a long wave view, the balancing of geo-political objectives against available resource. Discretion and a sense of proportion, in short, should have been the watchwords. But these are not known to the Egalitarian Fantasists.

There are three major forces affecting the redrawing of historic national boundaries. The first is the centralism of the European Union which is sparking the second, secessionist tendencies within national states and leading to the third, the redrawing of Cold War battle lines between the United States, on the one hand, and Russia and China on the other with Europe hovering in undisguised confusion in the middle.

And so emerges the beginning of the new tri-polar world.

On the one hand stands China and its newly-found friendship with Russia and the other members of the Bric nations. India swims in the same waters. This alliance brings in large swathes of South East Asia and dominions such as Australia.

On the other resides North America, the South American success nations, Japan, South Korea and the Sunni Kingdoms, the latter currently successful not because of innate capacity but the coincidental benefit of enormous natural resources.

Europe, bureaucratic, protectionist, unproductive, subsidy-driven, locked into a failing union and flailing currency, will slowly fracture into a success northern region and a struggling southern one, a place that will eventually be visited by wealthy Chinese and Russians on grand tours, just as the British did in the 18th century. They will no doubt ask the same question: how did these great empires end like this? Britain still has to make its choices.

The Fantasy is at the root of the current waves of unprecedented social protest sweeping the developing world: the Arab Spring, Turkey, Brazil, India, Egypt, Ukraine and so on. Remarkably, these protestors are not the desperately poor but the newly-enfranchised middle classes, particularly the youth. Strip away the obvious and legitimate protests against corruption and state incompetence, and the single thread uniting all these protests is a demand for *more and better*, more and better than they are currently getting and more and better than their societies can deliver or afford at their current state of development.

Why the particular vigour of these social revolutions based on fantastically rising expectation? The one reason, obviously, is the technical mobilising capacity of social media, the ultimate institution of power without a scintilla of responsibility. The other answer is the Egalitarian Fantasy and its long reach to all parts of the globe.

It was the consequences of the Egalitarian Fantasy that generated the unsustainable and vast consumption-based societies of the developed world. That in turn prompted developing world countries to grow unbalanced export-led economies while simultaneously suctioning industrial jobs out of the developed world. It was a consequence of the Fantasy that Western banks extended unconscionable levels of credit to emerging markets so as to fund the creation of internal consumerism to acquire Western luxury exports and, conversely, led ultimately to emerging markets investing heavily in developed world countries, including US property.

Again, it was the Egalitarian Fantasy that drove the collapse of Western competitiveness through the rising social cost of labour, brought economic slow-down and acute social tensions to developing world countries. And, lastly, it was the Fantasy that imposed developed world political ideas on countries caught in the terrible paradox of rapid economic growth managed by decayed traditional political systems. The Facebook street mobs in the developing world are demanding levels of immediate personal satisfaction that the developed world took centuries to attain --- and a short six decades to lose thanks to the Egalitarian Fantasy.

These are demands that cannot be met in the short-term and if there was one lesson from events in Syria, China, Russia and Turkey in 2013, it was that the leaders called upon to manage their highly diverse and deeply stressed societies could draw no benefit from compromise or prevarication. The Egalitarian Fantasy confronted these leaders with an all or nothing option: retain power or capitulate to the Fantasy, with the certain prospect of chaos and a seat in the dock of the Fantasy's International Court of Human Justice in the event of the latter.

The baleful and naïve role played by the Egalitarian Fantasy in undermining the developed world's prestige and self-confidence are brutally apparent. Iraq, Afghanistan, the Arab Spring, Syria, Egypt, Ukraine, all the Western interventions were premised on the belief that *they* were like *us* and that just given the chance these liberated countries would install models of Western democratic order. Now, after the oceans of blood, money and devastation, the more reasoned elements of the developed world have been forced to accept that they are not just like us, they are different; genetically, biologically, emotionally, culturally different, and they are best placed to settle *their* societies on *their* terms.[4]

This raises its own problems. What if *their* solution constitutes a real and patent danger to *our* interests, whether economic or security? One thing we now know with dread certainty: trying to deal with the issue by converting these countries to Western liberal concepts of democracy does not work. Thousands of dead American and British servicemen and hundreds of thousands of dead civilians have proved it.

The alternative of using brutal, 19th century gun boat diplomacy is just not available. Developed world nations, infused by the Egalitarian Fantasy, are too squeamish to accept this and in any case, the "judicialisation" of the military through endless court inquiries into their conduct in foreign wars, has made them impotent. Thus critical Western security interests remain in a no-win situation: vast military resources unable to effectively deploy in asymmetrical warfare because of "human rights" restraints, judicial second-guessing and internal security agencies hobbled by civil rights measures. In such a stalemate, terrorists prosper.[5]

The public was well ahead of the politicians on this one. In the UK, through its Parliament, it forced its Government in 2014 not to intervene in the Syrian sectarian violence on the side of a polyglot rebel army of religious secessionists, terrorists and bandits. They *knew* there was no point. In the US, President Obama shrewdly suggested putting intervention to Congress, knowing it would also reject it. When a far bigger test arose in 2014, the need to support a pro-EU Ukrainian Government that had with EU instigation seized power from a legitimate pro-Russian government through threat of violence, there was no appetite to militarily confront a justifiably outraged Russia.

Again, when Jihadist forces invaded Iraq from Syria in June 2014, recapturing ground that had been paid for in the blood of British and American soldiers a scant five years before, there was no public or political mood for going back in strength. There was just no point. In the end the West had to rely on Play Station bombing interventions and desperate attempts to arm local militia, any militia, including ones previously deemed terrorist, to confront the monster the West had created through its own naiveté.

Indeed, one of the most interesting developments in the 21st century will most certainly be the growth of state-sponsored private military formations, mustered to deal with immediate security threats and deployed to distant parts on the loosest rein possible to achieve outcomes formal western armies are either unable or unwilling to secure. If this sounds familiar, it should. It was the way European potentates achieved their ends through centuries. Yet again, the Egalitarian Fantasy and its effect on the confidence of the Western military, takes us giant leaps backwards.

Beyond all these superficial and volatile social and political movements and concerns, however, the Egalitarian Fantasy and its consequences have delivered vacuums of power that trigger deep and certain currents that presage the restoration of age old centres of power based on historic pools of genetic and biological capacity.

Thus we have a still vigorous America turning inwards and outwards to the Pacific --- it has given up on a weak, self-indulgent, fractious Europe with no iron in the soul and a hopelessly embattled Middle East; Europe resolving into its component power core (German speaking

Europe, the Baltic states, Scandinavia and the lowlands versus the rest); France, the proud yet often abject suitor to northern power; an independent Britain, wary of entrapment in lasting alliances other than America and possibly Northern Europe; a resentful and still significant Russia competing against the West for influence in central Europe and Asia; central Europe itself divided into the west-inclined success nations (mostly Catholic or Protestant) and the east-inclined less successful ones (mostly Muslim or Orthodox); a resurgent Ottoman influence in the Middle East and Balkans under an increasingly despotic Turkish leadership; a clear divide between Sunni and Shia potentates in the Middle East and a risen and inscrutable power in the Far East.

All of these regions, without exception, are prone to rebellious minorities, sometimes violent contests along historic borders and secessionist tendencies, in Europe's case made ironically worse by the European Union's financial support for regions. In its bid to diminish the power of national sovereigns by promoting regions it has unleashed one of the oldest and most dangerous dynamics of European history --- secession.[6]

Does this sound familiar? Of course it is. Substitute China for Japan, replace old imperial monarchies with the German-dominated European Union and add the artificial and political construct of the Israeli state and one has the essential power balance that has characterized the global international scene for centuries. *Plus ça change, plus c'est la même chose...* And, oh yes, periodically one European force attempts to dominate all others on the continent --- a Caesar or a Charlemagne, a Napoleon or a Hitler --- and is inevitably defeated by the combined weight of assorted nationalistic faiths. Today, it is the European Commission (one of three main institutions involved in the EU) seeking to tread this tiresomely familiar path.

THE PUSH BACK BEGINS

But nothing is static for long. The developed world will change, is changing and can only but change. The Egalitarian Fantasy has very nearly run its course. The push back has begun. The regressive and passe egalitarianism of the 20th Century Old Left is now on the back foot. Confronted by both science and empirical evidence, the old forms of unqualified and naive egalitarianism is under sustained attack.

The link between price and value of labour is being restored, brutally in some cases, and it is affecting investment bankers as much as it is car park attendants. The disposable income of the average UK household was by 2012 back to 2003 levels: a decade of income growth wiped out as cost of labour realigned to the value of labour.[1]

So too is the break between qualification and competence being repaired: apprenticeships and work experiences are back in vogue. The madcap rush for university places has slowed: young people are now considering trades. Again, useless qualifications in "media studies" and other nonsenses are on the wane. Job-seekers want qualifications better able to find them jobs and pay their bills. The number of British people who claim they are under considerable pressure to be successful and earn money has nearly doubled in five years. All this is good.[2]

Affirmative action is under review in most countries. An exemplar has to be post-liberation South Africa where a black majority government has pumped billions of dollars of resource into various affirmative action and "empowerment" projects to advance members of the black majority after years of discrimination under the apartheid system. In September 2014, the head of the South African Chamber of Commerce released research showing that the proportion of young black people in the age group 25-34 years in skilled positions was less than before liberation 20 years earlier.[3]

In Malaysia, affirmative action programmes aimed at the indigenous population caused an unnecessarily high emigration of high-skilled Chinese and Indian-descended Malaysians. By 2015, 70% of Malaysians were agreed that the bumiputra programme had achieved little more than encourage dependency. Similar mixed outcomes dogged India's "reservation" policies to advance its lowest Castes.

Such experiences, replicated in many other countries which had embarked on affirmative action programmes, signalled yet again that throwing huge amounts of money at social problems was no guarantee of success and that there are many other factors which stand between deprivation and achievement. The heavy financial subsidy that societies paid to employ people from targeted groups merely on "potential" must logically be reduced in the future. This is a tacit yet unacknowledged acceptance of the reality of innate capacity.

The link between price and value of assets is being restored: the average American had by 2012 lost 45% in the value of their assets compared to 2008, overwhelmingly due to the plunge in house prices.[4] This savage realignment has at least allowed the US to enjoy a return to growth, even if only half of that enjoyed in the two decades prior to 2008.

The days of the classical welfare state are numbered as benefits are cut and the size of the state pushed back. The NGO sectors must follow, thus placing under threat the numerous fantasy jobs and fantasy work. The engineered miasma of fear, guilt and insecurity which pervades developed world societies and has given them so much of their contours of anxiety, disillusionment and corrosive envy, must in the medium term be contained and challenged.. The era of the "expert" is over in the popular mind: that mind has been fed too much nonsense over too long a period to believe as credulously as it once did.

The drive for vast legions of fiercely competitive academics and researchers to publish --- publish anything as long as it will catch a headline – must surely now recede. Already, research into research (yes, we have reached that point) has shown that very nearly 80% of what is published in newspapers as preliminary findings is subsequently withdrawn, never validated, not followed up or simply proved wrong.[5] And with this realignment must follow a much fiercer public evaluation of traditional media and the damaging role it has played in uncritically promoting the cause of the supercrisis.org corporates for decades.[6]

The suffocating burden of the accumulative generosity of successive generations of western politicians is most intensely felt in the provisions made for the care of the elderly: over 90% of social welfare spend in developed states is devoted to caring for the ballooning numbers in this sector. Tentative corrections are underway --- extending retirement age by as much as four years, ending gold plated retirement plans and insisting that a wider group of people contribute to the costs of their old age.

As pensions lose value, accommodation costs rise and earnings potential falter, we are seeing another resurrected phenomenon: the extended family hearth. Rich developed world countries are following the model of their poorer neighbours, inter-generational households are again becoming common. In the UK alone, the number of households with at least six occupants had risen by a quarter in five years.[7] Not only does this mean a better utilization of resources, sharing of household income and division of work, but it also re-establishes the core of the stable family unit.

Already, there are encouraging signs of a return to the values which made great nations once great. The benefits of marriage, fidelity, education, duty, faith or loyalty to institutions are returning, at least amongst the success classes and those who aspire to success. Attitude surveys of young people in the United States and United Kingdom are returning the surprising finding that today's young people drink less, smoke less, take fewer drugs, fall pregnant as teenagers less, have fewer casual sexual liaisons and are less condoning of infidelity than their parent's generation. They are also more sceptical of politicians' motives and less supportive of political parties, although they do rally around specific issues which appeal to their basic instincts of fairness. They doubt that institutions can provide them with a happy life.[8]

So, the good thing is that young people seem to be more abstemious and questioning and doubting about the ability of the welfare state to care for them. The bad news is that they are generally becoming less genetically intelligent, less fit, more isolated and less socially adept. The big question, the really big one, is whether they have become more willing to accept responsibility for their own lives or have they just slumped into a mind-set of cynical indifference and scepticism; on a life support system maintained by uninterrupted 180 character injections of inanity from Twitter or 'liked ' comments on Facebook, interspersed with spasms of social conscience about whatever "crisis" is currently trending.

A return to core conservative and traditionalist values must thus not be overstated. But there does appear to be a beginning of the acceptance of what science is now telling us: the key to human success is not just cognitive skills measured by IQ scores but genetic non-cognitive skills defined as character and described as grit, perseverance, self-discipline, integrity and loyalty. Recognise those? Yes, after years of denigration by the Egalitarian Fantasy Victorian values are back; just as a world order based on genetic pools of competence is again beginning to be vaguely discernible.[9]

Across the developed world, a push-back against the sour and crippling legacies of the Egalitarian Fantasy seems to be taking place. It is an uneven process, more identifiable in some countries than others depending on circumstances and the willingness of leaders to address the disease rather than gnaw at its symptoms. Everywhere it is characterised by irony and paradox.

In the United State a redistributive President chose to save the banks and throw the people to the wolves. Foreclosures and job losses were horrific. Yet of all the countries of the developed world, the US is poised to rebound the quickest in terms of sustainable growth. In the UK, a Conservative-led government chose to save the people, despite its rhetoric of "austerity", and yet do hardly anything about the banks. They opposed EU measures to cap banker bonuses and implement a banking union. They have arrested perhaps three bankers over the multiple multi billion frauds perpetrated since 2007/8. The power of the City of London has risen not diminished and this largely because the UK has many fewer manufacturing jobs to offer its population.[10] It condemned itself to a slower than necessary recovery. In France, a narrow Socialist victory, has ensured national amnesia and denial, guaranteeing the painful economic degradation of a major nation and the inexorable rise of a right wing nationalist-led backlash.

In the European Union, hopelessly hog-tied by the implausibility of its single currency, the push-back against the legacy of the Egalitarian Fantasy has perforce been most severe in the marginal countries: Greece, Italy and Spain;

they have no options. It is a test of the steely German determination to maintain a single currency in which they can trade their exports at a 30% discount.

Attempts by the European Central Bank to stimulate ailing southern economies and pump-prime consumption through quantitative easing may mean in the short-term the saving of the common currency. In the long term it promises a continuing weakening of European competitiveness and a certain march to the unanswered yet richly historic question: to what extent will the ordinary people of sovereign European nations be prepared to surrender the political and cultural independence they have fought for centuries to defend, to support a faltering common currency and a disconnected, authoritarian and disdainful European political class? Not much longer is the answer. Across Europe in 2014 increasingly powerful conservative, traditional and nativist political parties grew in opposition to the EU's contemptuous and anti-democratic processes, its one-world delusions, its Egalitarian Fantasy.

LAST THOUGHTS

Early in this Essay I sought to canvas the rapid progress that has been made in extending our understanding of the essence of our physical and mental being, thanks to the discovery of DNA and exercises such as the Human Genome Project and all that has flowed from it.

The information and illumination has been breath taking. From institutions as diverse as Kings College London, Edinburgh University in Scotland, Toronto's York University and the Centre for Addiction and Mental Health, the Universities of Oxford, Exeter, Birmingham, University College London and Sussex in the UK, the Universities of Pennsylvania, Duke, Harvard, New Mexico, Brown, John Hopkins and the Massachusetts Institute of Technology in the US, the Los Angeles Biomedical Research Institute, the University of Georgia's centre for Family Research, the Max Plank Institute in Germany, the Karolinska Institute in Sweden, the National University of Singapore, the International Institute for Applied Systems Analysis in Vienna and many, many more, come new waves of research and reporting that takes us every moment a step closer to better understanding the mystery and the mastery of the human being.

The list of scientists who are engaged in this process is too long to name but to them must go the credit for having had the courage to stand up against the often intimidating orthodoxies defended for decades by the Left which sought to subject all knowledge, all understanding, to the iron constraints of ideology. I do not expect the scientists to agree with my interpretation of its social, political and economic impact. That alone is my responsibility.

The research from so many diverse points does not perfectly accord (when has it ever in science) but the overwhelming weight of it reasserts the importance of genetic, epigenetic and biological influences in our lives. The 20th Century Left wing mythologies about the mind and society, the utopian visions of a world of perfect equality, the Egalitarian Fantasy, are challenged, weighed and found wanting. The 21st century opens a new world --- at this point neither brave nor settled, but unmistakeably exciting.

The reality of innate differences in capacity between individuals and groups is now widely accepted. The failure of naïve and costly egalitarian policies is painfully evident. Yet nowhere is the root cause of the crisis addressed openly. That is still a bridge too far. So we focus on the symptoms; iniquitous bankers, colluding corporates, unfeeling bureaucracies, lying misery and guilt industries, indolent benefit classes and sponging immigrants. There is much to recommend all of this but it is still not enough.

We are still too afraid to contemplate the cure when it involves a frank acceptance that we are not innately equal; that lack of success in some individuals and groups is an unavoidable condition; that mass investments in social welfare is pointless; that poverty, as the Bible tells us, will always be with us; that it is not the value creators who are the enemy of a just society but the value consumers and destroyers, fashioned by the left-liberal consensus; that the lashing together of unequal people, whether in class-rooms, electorates, alliances of states, currency unions or anywhere else is a ticket to crisis and frustration; that egalitarianism results in an underlying deep unfairness to both those who can and want to get ahead and those who cannot get ahead and would be best served by an honest and caring acknowledgement of that reality.

Crucially, we are afraid to confront the fact that our present crisis is not due to a lack of egalitarianism but to its surfeit; that our sin has not been our failure to reduce inequality, but our refusal to accommodate ourselves to its reality; that the current crisis of Western modernity is not because we have not done enough to end inequality, but because the measures we have taken to reach a utopian foreland have been deeply misguided.

The crisis of the 21st century is one of great urgency and peril. Why? Six short reasons.

One, the ticket to play in the super successful class in terms of genetic intelligence has just shot up. Technological advance, complexity of organization, scale of enterprise and globalization has seen to that. The numbers able to play is thus small, and shrinking as a proportion of the whole.

Two, the second category, let us call them the middle classes for convenience, is getting the worst comparative deal in history. Not only is their opportunity for advancement more limited than perhaps even in feudal times, but they are also taking real economic pain, being expected to carry heavy tax burdens while enduring depressed earnings and diminishing disposal incomes, all of this a direct consequence of the Egalitarian Fantasy. The fortunes of their children will be even bleaker and that realisation could spark a conflagration.

Three, the third category, let us for decorum's sake's use the BBC's term the "precariat", are the most at-risk category. The Egalitarian Fantasy has ensured that although they may be growing faster numerically than the other two categories, they are becoming less fit physically and mentally by the year as the research published above attests. Their prospects of finding employment, even at the most menial level, have been severely diminished thanks to the Egalitarian Fantasy.

Four, all this would perhaps have been manageable under circumstances of significant wealth creation and disbursement, but the Egalitarian Fantasy has handicapped this capacity and has simultaneously created a hugely inflated sense of entitlement and expectation at all levels of the society --- expectations that are economically unattainable other than in the long term.

Five, this has added a particular vehemence to the nature of political contestation which is now putting the century-old institutions of modern democratic government in *all* developed world countries under intense and perhaps unsustainable pressure.

Six, finally, the history of the developed world has been an unbroken record of long wave social and economic advancement of all levels of societies for centuries (give or take a few violent irruptions and reversals). That, for all but a few has now hit pause. The situation is worsening while that of the wealthiest, what in the United States has been dubbed the Super Zips after their elite residential address codes, is soaring.

The survival of the developed world's existence depends on change, for we cannot continue in the new era as we did in the old. We can no longer pursue the Fantasy; we do not have the resources for it. We cannot hold to our old self-indulgent, indolent ways; there is no time for it. We need to accept that the worst form of social injustice is to expect swathes of our people to behave beyond their genetic limitations; to attain goals not of their making or within their grasp and particularly not to expect that they can do so with the degraded and discarded tools provided by the Left and their egalitarian cohorts.

Right now, there are six issues which should grip us all, at a political, social and emotional level.

First, we must accept the reality of genetic and biological difference between individuals and groups; neither to revel in that reality nor to exploit it but to understand and mediate it.

Second, we must accept that genetic competence is at a premium. We must use all our resources to identify it, wherever it may be, and promote it. Only thus can 21st Century Western societies be secured.

The tools are available. Professor Anne Bowcock, Professor of Cancer Genomics at Imperial College, believes babies will be genetically sequenced from birth "within our lifetime". She is of course referring primarily to screening for disease but it could just as well be done for a range of cognitive and non-cognitive capabilities and traits.

Third, we can no longer rely on an ever diminishing base of value and tax creators to support us all. There is work ahead for everybody. Those who have lived on the sweat of other's labour must be put back to work.

Fourth, we can no longer tolerate a system which consigns those that have neither the cognitive nor non-cognitive ability to succeed in a fiercely competitive world to be shuffled off to some limbo of state supported dependency and manipulation for the mere purpose of multiplying jobs for others. They must be given protection, dignity and work.

Fifth, finally, modern democracy is no longer fit for purpose. We need to find alternatives that put influence back in the hands of those ordinary people who through their labour, self-sufficiency, sense of personal accountability, community investment and financial stake make tomorrow happen for all of us. We need political leadership that leads: not cravenly follows the worst instincts of its society.

The scientific groundwork has been laid. The issues are clearly grasped. The debate, so long suppressed, needs to begin. Then, only then, will we be able to address the most fundamental question of all: on what basis does a rational and fair society, fully aware of the genetic frailty of sections of its community, decide whom is competent to participate in the critical business of government and on what terms. However it is decided, it will be the end of classic liberalism and welfarism. It will be the end of the Egalitarian Fantasy and the 60 year cul de sac into which a once vibrant developed world has been led.

The existing national institutional structures, although scarred, damaged and demeaned, still mercifully provide the platforms for a peaceful reformation. But they are under enormous strain. How much longer can they survive the upheavals caused by a failed egalitarian ideology kept on life-support system only by powerful, disconnected and vested interests?

It is surely not an exaggeration to observe that a hinge point in modern Western democratic history has been reached.

SCIENCE VERSUS THE EGALITARIAN FANTASY

1. Asbury and Robert Plomin's G is for Genes (2014). This focuses on the role of genes in determining educational outcomes but has wider implications. Genes, for example, are held to account for about half of the differences in people in terms of cognitive ability and 40% in terms of achievement. It is also held to account for at least 30% of the difference in income levels of individuals.

   Research estimates that genetic heritability accounts for between 60% and 70% of the difference in skills as basic as reading, writing and mathematics. Genes can explain approximately half of the difference between people in the educational qualifications they gain and 40% of the variability in the status of jobs they do. It also finds these genetic influences are more important for achievement than environmental impacts like family or school. (Asbury & Plomin: 2014).

   More on this subject comes from Edinburgh University's project, published in the *Journal of Personality* which assessed 800 pairs of twins and found a very significant role for genes in determining a range of traits which enable people to succeed. Professor Bates, who led the research, was quoted as saying: "Previously, the role of the family and the environment around the home often dominated people's ideas about what affected psychological well-being. However, this work highlights a much more powerful influence from genetics. If you think of things that people are born with you think of social status or virtuoso talent, but this is looking at what we do with what we have got. The biggest factor we found was self-control. There was a big genetic difference in (people's ability) to restrain themselves and persist with things when they got difficult and react to challenge in a positive way." (*The Daily Telegraph: May 19 2012*)

2. Matt Asbury and Plomin (2014) find that the effects of genetic heritability become more pronounced as a person grows older. This theme is extensively explored in Matt Ridley's superb *Genome* (1999)

3. Nicholas Wade's *A Troublesome Inheritance (2014)* is one of the most courageous attempts to deal with the reality of genetically based differences between racial groups and makes the point that it is absurd to deny that the human genome is not in a process of constant evolution and that different races have not developed independently of each other in the last 5 000 to 30 000 years.

4. *The Sports Gene: Talent, Practice and the Truth About Success* by David Epstein (2014) is an engaging read which emphasises the crucial role that genes play in sports excellence, something that the Egalitarian Fantasists have been loath to concede happens also in human intellectual virtuosity.

5. Nicholas Wade vis

6. Epstein vis

7. Socio economic status (SES) is influenced by genes as well as experiences. The relationship between SES and achievement is partly genetic in origin, explains Asbury and Plomin (2014). The two things are linked to a person's DNA. "This means that the children of parents who themselves did not succeed at school and went on to achieve low status in society are likely to resemble their parents as much for genetic reasons as environmental reasons. In essence, it is likely that children growing up in low-income families... are genetically as well as environmentally vulnerable." (Pg133)

    Research by Dr Martha Farrah of the University of Pennsylvania augmented by Drs Schamberg and Evans of Cornell showed that the working memories of children raised in poverty were less than those of middle-class children --- 8.5 items held in memory versus

9.4. This may seem a small differential but it is critical to levels of executive function. This would explain the numerous studies which show children of working class children more or less keep pace with their middle class peers for about two years then rapidly fall behind. Working memories are not able to keep up with the additional information load.

8. *A Troublesome Inheritance* by Nicholas Wade (2014)

9. Irving L Janis *Groupthink (Second Edition)(1972)*

10. *Not in Our Genes* by R C Lewontin, Steven Rose and Leon J Kamin (Pantheon Books: 1984) Pg 267. In 1979 philosopher Michael Ruse attempted in his *Sociobiology: Sense or Nonsense* to apply the rigorous techniques of philosophical analysis to the debate. It was a sterling effort but again one could not but be painfully aware of the huge gaps in basic knowledge that bedevilled both the debate and its analysis.

11. Much work has been done on the huge differences in average national intelligences and an accepted matrix of 108 nations is now available. The hierarchy places Singapore and South Korea at the top at 107, followed by Chinese at 105 and so on down to Australian Aboriginals with a score of 64. Broadly speaking, Asians are at the 100+ mark, Europeans

and North Americans around the 100, Arabs and South Americans around the 90 mark and West and Eastern Africans at the 80 and southern Africans in the 60's and 70's. Other research puts Ashkenazi Jews at the very top with a score of 108. Richard Lynn and Gerhard Meissenberg in an article in *Intelligence* (38) of 2010 establish the key linkages between average national intelligence and educational achievement.

12. On December 13 1994, 52 researchers in the fields of intelligence testing published in The Wall Street Journal a statement setting out 25 conclusions regarding their understanding of the status of the debate about intelligence testing and race. After reaffirming the credibility of current intelligence testing models and the importance of intelligence in human achievement, they observed that heritability estimates range from 0.4 to 0.8, indicating genetics plays a bigger role than environment in creating IQ differences. The bell curve for whites is centred roughly at IQ 100, American blacks at roughly 85 with Hispanics roughly midway. They also found that difference between the races is still substantial when corrected for socio-economic class.

In his book, *A Troublesome Inheritance (2014)*, Nicholas Wade, goes further in exploring the antecedents to the patently different social behaviours of different racial groups. In his words: "The thesis presented here assumes......that there is a genetic component to human social behaviour; that this component, so critical to human survival, is subject to evolutionary change and has indeed evolved over time; that the evolution in social behaviour has necessarily proceeded independently in the five major races and others: and that slight evolutionary differences in social behaviour underlie the differences in social institutions prevalent among the major human populations. (Pg242)

13. Asbury and Plomin (2014) for example identify self-confidence as having a significant impact on academic achievement and together with IQ is the best predicator of success. Fifty one per cent of the difference between the Twins Early Development Study (TEDS) twins (at 9 years of age) in terms of self-perceived ability in academic subjects was explained by their genes. Self confidence is at least as heritable as IQ and almost as heritable as achievement.

Research supports the notion that achievement is not solely based on IQ. There are other traits, equally genetically based, which account for it. This has led to the development of the concept of Emotional Intelligence (eQI), the range of attributes, disciplines and traits, the presence of which make individuals more sociable and able to interact with fellow humans. The evidence so far is that eQI fairly closely matches

IQ as a measurement of propensity to success, or lack of it. An early work on the subject is Daniel Goleman's *Emotional Intelligence (1996.)*

14. Paul Tough in his book *How Children Succeed: Grit, Curiosity and the Hidden Power of Character* (Houghton Mifflin Harcourt: 2013) draws together extensive research showing the impact that lack of non-cognitive skills have on the life's chances of poor people. This he largely attributes to the effects of epigenetics and the impairment of executive function in certain children. This is part of the reason why participants in programmes such as the Knowledge is Power programme in the Bronx amongst poor Afro-Americans and Hispanics fail at college level while showing progress at lower levels of education. He claims that a focus on developing non-cognitive skills has yielded good results, although of course the unanswered question is whether the success cases achieve because of the programme or because they had the genotype to succeed in the first place i.e. positive genotype-environment association.

Bryan Jeremy, in a PhD student dissertation for Ohio University in 2005 sought to establish the relationship between student leadership and eQI. He found significant differences between white and black respondents. Black students scored high on assertiveness but lower on measures for self-actualisation, stress management, impulse control, general mood and happiness. Whites also scored higher in "modelling the way" and "challenging the process".

15. Research by Dr Ragini Verma of the University of Pennsylvania, published in *Proceedings of the National Academy of Sciences: 2013* suggests the brains of men and women are wired differently. Men's brains have more nerve fibres and women more grey matter. Women also have better interlinked halves of the brain. These differences lead to different attributes which are grounded initially in genetics but develop as individuals grow. The research proves structural differences in the brains of the genders and backs a growing body of research that men and women do indeed behave differently, respond differently to stimuli and have different innate strengths and weaknesses.

Earlier research carried out by Marco Del Guidice and published in *Public Library of Science One (2012)* suggested women were inherently more sensitive, warm apprehensive, self-reliant and tense than men. Men were more emotionally stable, dominant, rule-conscious, vigilant and open to change.

Other intriguing research carried out by Jonathan Wai, Martha Putallaz and Matthew Akel of Duke

University of North Carolina, reviewed in *Current Directions in Psychological Science (October 30 2012,)* found males outnumbered females 13 to one in the top 0.01% of maths scores in 1980 in the US. By the early 1990's this was down to four to one. Then improvement in female scores ceased. The implications are obvious: genotype ensured the improvement of female performance as gender stereotypes changed until the point was reached where genetic difference was dominant and perhaps irreducible, impervious to social intervention.

Research by Daniella Weber, lead researcher in a 32 000 subject project by the International Institute for Applied Systems Analysis in Vienna and published in the *Proceedings of the National Academy of Science* in July 2014, reported clear and unmistakeable differences between men and women in such skills as episodic memory and numeracy, despite the narrowing of the IQ gap between the genders during the 21st Century. She observed that there was no reason to expect that all cognitive gender differences will diminish but if men and women had equal levels of education than one should expect elimination of the gaps in certain specific areas.

16. A fascinating hit on this has been the work of Gregory Clark in *The Son Also Rises (2014)*, an economist at

the University of California, Davis who uses family names to track the replication of wealth and thus success through family dynasties. He found in his studies of Swedes that 70% to 80% of a family's social status is transmitted from generation to generation. The Egalitarian Fantasists would deny genetic determination in any of this

17. Research done by Peter Hatemi of Pennsylvania University and Rose McDermott of Brown University, published in *Trends in Genetics (2012)* which shows a significant genetic influence in the political attitudes people take in life.

18. Research by the Universities of Exeter and Birmingham, in a report for the Office of the Children's Commissioner, *Nobody made the Connection (2014)* found a prevalence of neurodisability in young people who offend, apart from finding a significant correlation in young offenders and speech and writing disabilities and also found evidence of significant brain trauma and malformation thus reinforcing the importance of hardware.

19. Leonard Mlodinow in his book *How Your Unconscious Mind Rules Your Behaviour* (2013) presents a compelling argument that the subconscious mind, rather than being the swamp of repressed memories as suggested by

Freud, is in fact a very sophisticated computer drawing on all sorts of inputs, some genetic, to guide individuals towards making appropriate decisions for survival. This includes classifying people into different groups, ethnic, racial or other, in order to assess them from a threat perspective.

20. The research is supported by psychologist David Brook's The Social Animal: *The Hidden Sources of Love, Character and Achievement (2011)* which argues much of human behaviour is conditioned from an early age and is subconscious. He places some emphasis on the cultural embedding of behaviour.

    A new area of research has opened up with neuromorphics --- the building of computers complex enough to simulate human brains. At least two multi-billion projects are underway in America and Europe to unlock the remaining secrets of the human brain, most importantly, to what extent is our brain pre-programmed.

21. An interesting book on the subject of evolutionary biology is Avi Tuschman's *Our Political Nature (2013).* His argument is that the key determinant in whether a person is of conservative or liberal political orientation does not relate primarily to rational economic self interest but to inherent genetic characteristics

deriving from deep-seated biological evolutionary influences. He estimates heritability in political orientation at about 40% to 60%: roughly in line with estimates of heritability for other capacities and traits.

22. *The Invisible History Of The Human Race* by Christine Kenneally (2014)

23. Professor Peter Saunders, Professor of Sociology at Sussex University, reported in *Civitas: 2010* on the studies on 11 year-olds in the 1958 age cohort which confirmed that IQ was by far the most important factor in future success. Further research by Professor Michael Zephur of the National University of Singapore into business school graduates also found that IQ was the greatest influencing factor in the future success of graduates.

24. Matt Ridley: *Nature versus Nurture* (2003)

25. The iconic sacrificial lambs on the altar of political correctness had to be Professors Arthur Jensen and Hans Eysenk, pilloried for daring to suggest there might be differences in intelligences between the races and that this might be heritable.

26. Steven Pinker, in his *The Blank State* (1997), comprehensively demolished most of the arguments of the

extremist environmentalists to re-assert the importance of genetics and biology, the innate human, in
creating character and personality.

27. Asbury and Plomin (2014)

28. Mosing, Miriam, *Psychological Science,* reported in *The Economist* July 5 – 11 2014.

29. David Epstein's *The Sports Gene* effectively captures this interplay between the hard and soft attributes which leads to sporting excellence by studying the achievements of a range of sporting heroes in various codes.

30. Asbury and Plomin (2014) find that the effects of genetic heritability become more pronounced as a person grows older. This theme is extensively explored in Matt Ridley's *Genome (1999)*

31. David Epstein: *The Sports Gene*: 2014

32. The field of behavioural epigenetics is still in its infancy and primarily directed at dealing with psychopathology and mental health issues. Our understanding of its impact on cognitive and non-cognitive abilities in both individuals and groups is growing exponentially. The best current textbook on the subject is Lyle Armstrong's Epigenetics (2014).

33. An overwhelming body of research now points to the very close correlation between genetic frailty and adverse external experiences in the parent. Research by the University of Pennsylvania's School of Veterinary Medicine published in *Proceedings of the National Academy of Sciences* (2013) showed the role of the enzyme OGT in transferring the effects of stress from a rat mother's placenta to an offspring. This enzyme triggered changes in more than 370 genes critical to the neurological development of brains.

34. Ibid

35. Work by Christopher Eppig of the University of New Mexico, published in *The Proceedings of The Royal Society* (2010) establishes the precise correlation between levels of disease within a country and the average national intelligence of that country. Without qualification, high disease burdens result in lower intelligence which in turns coincides with higher levels of social, political and economic dysfunction. Such dysfunction, of course, militates against dealing with the core issues propagating disease. And so the cycle continues.

36. Some ground-breaking work by Professor Art Petronis of the Krembil Family Epigentics Laboratory at the Centre for Addiction and Mental Health in Toronto

confirmed the effects of meythylation on mental stability and addictive behaviour.

Research by Virender Rehan of the Los Angeles Biomedical Research Institute on rats indicates that nicotine effects are passed on through epigenetic processes to offspring and grand offspring.

37. Work by Dr Clare Llewellyn of the Epidemiolgy and Public Health Department at the University College of London finds that 30% of the body weight of a child is down to genes and could be greater if the research is extended to look at rarer genetic mutations that cause obesity.

38. Dr Martha Farrah, University of Pennsylvania, and Drs Schamberg and Evans of Cornell (vis)

39. The best popular definition of epigenetic change was to be found in *The Economist* article *Baby Blues: July 23 2011): Epigenetics is a type of gene regulation that can be passed from cells to its daughters. The most common mechanism is methylation. This attaches methyl groups (a carbon atom and three hydrogens) to either adenine or cytosine, two of the four chemical bases that form the alphabet of DNA, depending on the gene involved. The consequence is to inactivate the gene being methylated. In the case of stress, previous studies have suggested that methylation of the gene which*

encodes glucocorticoid receptors is important. Glucocorticoid receptors relay signals from stress hormones in the blood cells. In particular, they do so in those regions of the brain that control behaviour. New- borns whose mothers suffered from depression while they were pregnant are known to have more highly methylated glucocorticoid receptor genes than others. The same is true of children who were abused when young. In infants, the level of glucocorticoid-receptor methylation is correlated with the release, in response to stress, of higher than normal hormones.

40. The longevity of epigenetic change is a subject of much research but as yet little outcome. Research by Jenny Tung and Yoav Gilad of the University of Chicago, published in the *Proceedings of the National Academy of Sciences: 2012* had some interesting re- sults from experimentations on female monkeys. Once the lower-status females had the social or- der reversed, their immune systems improved sug- gesting a reversibility of epigenetic change. The finding is open to challenge. Merely having bet- ter access to food would improve immune systems. Besides, the researchers achieved their result by changing the social hierarchy by simply removing the senior levels. Humans have tried that often. It is called revolution and its benefits are patchy, to say the least.

41. Asbury and Plomin (2014) find that IQ is the best single behavioural predicator of future success that we currently have. While genes may contribute as little as 20% to 30% to children's IQ in preschool, the influence grows with age. We need to accept, however, that IQ and achievement is not the same thing. This accounts for the mixed results of early learning programmes in the US and the UK for disadvantaged children. While they undoubtedly give a boost to children's IQ at an early stage it does not necessarily last. To find the answer why it is worth turning again to Paul Tough's book (see above: *How Children Succeed: Grit, Curiosity and the Hidden Power of Character* (Houghton Mifflin Harcourt: 2013).

42. Nicholas Wade's *A Troublesome Inheritance (2014)* ventures into the fraught territory of race and crime. He reports on the discovery of the role of the gene MAO-A which contains promoters which produce an enzyme called mono-amine oxidase. A series of research projects found that the lower the number of promoters, the more aggressive the personality; the disposition of promoters varied between different racial groups and, finally, five per cent of African American males in the sample had low promoter numbers compared to 0.1% in the Caucasian population. Wade is careful to raise all the usual disclaimers --- research still

to be validated, perhaps other unfound genes which promote aggression in Caucasians, environmental factors such as poverty --- but the link between genes and crime statistics is at the very least, intriguing.

43. Extraordinary progress has been made on gene therapy. At present it is mostly focused on augmenting defective genes with new ones. But the new process called CRISPR-Cas9 editing, promises the ability to repair broken DNA. It is now focussed on the field of curative medical gene therapy but very soon will have wider application for cognitive and even non-cognitive defects in humans and even holds the possibility of genetic editing to change the genomes of whole populations.

44. Paul Tough: *How Children Succeed: Grit, Curiosity and the Hidden Power of Character* (2013)

45. An apparent contradiction between rising IQ levels and declining genetic intelligence levels is explained by the fact that IQ is indeed influenced by external factors. Professor James Flynn in his *Rising IQ in the 21st Century (Cambridge University Press:2012)* argues that the advent of women to the working world and thus modernity, undoubtedly improved aggregate female IQ levels in the developed world to the point where they are equal to men. But there they have stabilised.

46. Professor James Flynn *Rising IQ in the 21ˢᵗ Century (Cambridge University Press: 2012)*

47. Flynn also points out the importance of the difference between g-loadings when determining IQ (which treats all ten subtests on the Wechsler scale as equal) and GQ (which weighs the subtests in accordance with their g-loading, i.e. contribution to general intelligence). This is important in determining intellectual capacity. Thus while blacks in the US have as a group somewhat closed the gap with whites in terms of IQ, they have not done so well in terms of GQ. As the levels of cognitive complexity rise, as they must in a globalised and technological age, the gap becomes more apparent. Flynn observes that blacks "have an unusual problem with complexity". (*Rising IQ in the 21ˢᵗ Century: 2012: pg 137*). He does not adduce any genetic influence in this.

48. Research by the University of Georgia's Centre for Family Research in the US surveyed 489 poor African American who had progressed up the social ladder and found material increases in their allostatic load --- a measure of blood pressure, body mass and stress hormones. This increase will have significant long-term effects on health.

49. Research by Zachary Kaminsky of John Hopkins University, Marlyand published in the *American Journal of Psychology (2014)*

50. Carl Degler, in his *In Search of Human Nature: The Decline and Revival of Social Darwinism in American Social Thought (1991)* perhaps best captures the hugely important shift which took place:

> "What the available evidence does seem to show is that ideology or a philosophical belief that the world could be a freer and more just place played a large part in the shift from biology to culture. Science, or at least certain scientific principles or innovative scholarship also played a role in the transformation, but only a limited one. The main impetus came from the will to establish a social order in which innate and immutable forces of biology played no role in accounting for the behaviour of social groups".

FIVE STAGES TO HISTORIC IRRELEVANCE

1. Organisation for Economic Cooperation and Development (OECD) statistics show the heavy cost the developed world paid to maintain the past,

current and future promise of the Egalitarian Fantasy. Between 2000 and 2013, social investment increased by an average of 16% of GDP in the OECD countries with the European countries showing increases of between a fifth and a quarter. The heaviest payer was France. By 2013, fully 35% of GDP was devoted to social spending. The EU alone was by 2014 accounting for 53% of all global welfare spend.

2. The Congressional Budget Office Report of December 18 2013 recorded that while Federal investment represented 30% of spend and six per cent of GDP in 1960, by 2012 it had halved. The International Monetary Fund in its March 2004 Public Investment and Fiscal Policy Report by the Fiscal Affairs Department, even then was recording catastrophic declines in public investment in physical infrastructure in the developed world.

3. The OECD 2011 Forum on Tracking Inequality reported the growing divide between the rich and the poor despite the trillions of national wealth invested in advancing the interests of the poor over six decades. In the first decade of the 21st Century alone, the incomes of the top 10% increased two per cent in real terms while those of the bottom 10% made only 1.4%. The Gini Coefficient --- a measure of inequality where an index of 0 means absolute equality and

1 means complete inequality --- increased 10% from 0.28 in 2000 to 0.31 in 2011. It may not sound a lot but in material terms it is huge.

4. The UK's Office for National Statistics' *Patterns of Social Mobility NS-SEC 1981-2001*, published in November 2012, and a number of other reports found that social mobility had staggered to a virtual halt by 2000. The Leftist interpretation was that the richer were getting richer by further rigging things against the poor. The real scenario, as argued in this Essay, was that the poorer were getting poorer because everything done by the Egalitarian Fantasy to relieve their plight simply made things worse.

5. Raj Chetty et al: Harvard University: Equality of Opportunity Project: January 2014

6. Gregory Clark: *The Son Also Rises: Surnames and the History of Social Mobility* (2014)

7. Ibid

8. Programme for International Student Assessment: OECD: 2013

9. Between 2000 and 2012, the number of British students gaining the prized AA+ grade in their GCSE

year had increased by 50%. The teachers insisted this was a result of their brilliant teaching but others, surveying the collapse of core skills as measured by PISA, were doubtful. Imposition of tougher marking standards under the Conservative Coalition in the UK in 2012 showed exactly how inflated the grades had become.

10. Research by Dr Felix Weinhardt of the London School of Economics with a sample of 15 000 children found that lower achieving children were better served by attending lower ranking schools rather than by being catapulted into high ranking schools. The research comprehensively demolished the Left wing mantra that high-achieving peers can automatically pull up lower achieving ones.

11. Research by economists Benjamin Tal and Emanuella Enenajor of CIBC World Markets showed that by 2014, university graduates in the US were earning on average 12% less than High School graduates when one takes into account the cost of their education. The unemployment rate amongst graduates was only 1.7% less than high school graduates. The implications were clear: tertiary education in the US was failing utterly to equip students with tradable work skills. The pattern was repeated throughout the developed world.

12. British Social Attitudes Survey 2013

13. *Studies in the Scope and Method of the Authoritarian Personality* was funded by the American Jewish Committee's Department of Scientific Research and the project was headed by Theodor Adorno, a member of the Frankfurt School of psychologists, philosophers and Marxists, most of whom fled to the US or the UK in the 1930's. The report purports to identify the key characteristics and origins of the "fascist" mind, the quality of "F" for fascist. It attributes it to the traits of conventionalism, submission to authority figures, aggressiveness, superstition, power and toughness, destructiveness and cynicism and sex. The work was criticised for methodological error, bias and its reliance on now outdated Freudian analysis. No matter, it became the handbook of the Left in its massively successful assault on traditionalist and conservative values and more than any other work contributed to the hollowing out of social identity in the developed world. The fact that the prototype fascists had been revolutionary socialists, not capitalists, got lost somewhere in the translation.

14. The growing gap between the cost of benefits to individuals versus economic contribution from individuals is captured in a slew of statistics. In the UK, for example, according to the Compendium of UK Statistics:

Economy's section on gross value add, by 2013 52% of households took out more in benefits than they put back in economic value. Ten years earlier it had been 42%. The proportion of people not paying Federal taxes in the US was 47% in 2013.

15. The Labour Costs Indexes from across the developed world has shown non-wage income --- pensions, paternity leave, sickness leave, maternity leave, national insurance --- have constantly outstripped real wage increases. From equivalence in 2000, the gap between wage and non-wage income had grown to 17% by 2014. By 2014, they accounted for 25% of total remuneration, according to Eurostat numbers. In Germany, non-wage costs increased from 55% of overall remuneration to 80% between 1972 and 1980 --- but at least Germany held onto its high-value export industries. This massive increase in the social cost of Western labour, I suggest, was the main precipitator of job flight beginning in the 1970's.

AND THE GROWTH OF FANTASY JOBS

1. National Council For Voluntary Organisations UK Society Alamanac

2. The growth in the number of people employed in the non-profit sector has been astonishing. Merely by illustration, 1.6m people were employed full-time in the UK in 2013. Local government employees were 2.3m. In the US, the number employed in the non-profit sector is 10.6 m compared to 2.7m in employment in the Federal Government. Ironically, the number of people employed by Government across the developed world has declined since the 2008 crisis only to be matched by a surge in employment in the neo-governmental sector as is reflected in the UK by statistics in the National Council for Voluntary Organisations UK Society Almanac. It has simply been a job redesignation exercise.

3. Official statistics from the UK Charities Commission indicate there were 161 266 voluntary organisations in the UK in 2013 and more than one million in the US, according to the US National Center for Charitable Statisics (NCCS) While many of these were worthwhile local initiatives, many were not: created to generate jobs not solve issues.

4. Daily Telegraph of August 14 2013 reported that the number of executives taking home six figure salaries in the UK's 14 biggest charities had risen by 60% in three years --- and this at a time of waning public subscription.

5. Jeremy Rifkind: The Rise of Anti-capitalism: New York Times. March 16 2014

6. National Council for Voluntary Organisations UK Society Almanac 2014

7. The Daily Telegraph. April 29 2014

8. National Council for Voluntary Organisations UK Society Almanac 2014

THE POVERTY FRANCHISE

1. Between 1981 and 2010, China unaided pulled 680m of its people out of extreme poverty. How did they do it? Not by the Egalitarian Fantasy.

2. The most common definition of poverty in developed countries is a household income less than half of the average national salary. In the case of the UK it amounts to £80 per week per person in a couple household versus a national average of £173. This at least was quantifiable. The latest wheeze by super-crisis.org was to introduce the concept of poverty as "social exclusion". Under this nebulous concept a child forced to share a bedroom or go without an

IPad or not have a television in their room can be considered "excluded" relative to its peers. Carried to its logical conclusion, the inability to access private educational institutions or live in super zip addresses may be considered "exclusionary". And by definition immigrants from poor countries are absolutely and totally "excluded". It is of course the Egalitarian Fantasy's mission to ensure that all these "excludeds" become "includeds".

3. By 2014 there were 9 000 charity shops in the UK alone turning annual profits of £290m. Many were no longer only selling donated and used goods but were retailing new goods as well. Small business lobbies repeatedly attempted to challenge the 80% rates exemptions the charities enjoyed or to limit sales of new products. All failed as supercrisis.org mobilised its considerable political and emotional clout in defence of the interests of its highly paid executives.

THE HEALTH FRANCHISE

1. Professor Chris Dowrick, Professor of Primary Medical Care, at Liverpool University, writing in the *British Medical Journal* in 2013 argues that over-diagnosis of mental illness is now a bigger threat than

under-diagnosis. The number of people diagnosed with mental illness in the UK doubled between 2002 and 2013. Dowrick believes millions are being treated for being simply sad.

2. The "condition" of Involutional Paranoia was first noted in 1907. It appeared to affect only elderly people who, remarkably, showed signs of concern about their finances, health and the ability to fend for themselves. It enjoyed a huge recovery in the latter part of the 20th century but waned after even the American Psychiatric Association refused to include it in its manual, the DSM-5, on the grounds that it was not a validly diagnosable condition. No matter, huge amounts of money had been made by then by supercrisis.org.

3. Myolgic Encephalomgelitis (ME) or Chronic Fatigue Syndrome (CFS) is almost unique in being a disease without a clear epidemiological basis although researchers from Columbia University did claim in 2015 to have found some immunological dysfunction in sufferers. It appears to strike women rather than men (six to one) and particularly either neurotic women or those of lower socio-economic status. Victims have however generally shown a remarkable capacity to recover from their chronic fatigue when it is suggested their problems are psychosomatic. One medical reporter for a major UK newspaper, Dr Max Pembroke,

himself a psychiatrist, was assailed by thousands of outraged victims through social media, displaying what he called an "astounding degree of paranoia and obsession" when he merely reported on the lack of an epidemiological basis to the condition. Eventually, he was given police protection, surely an indication of the frightening power of the ability of the volatile fringe minorities to mobilise social media to incite intimidation. (Reported in The Daily Telegraph, September 24 2012)

4. Of the 1.25m US men and women who served in Iraq and Afghanistan, more than 500 000 subsequently received compensation from the Veterans Administration, many for psychiatric problems, by far the largest number of veterans relying on aid in the history of the US military. The sheer scale raised not only questions about the psychological capacity of post modern Western people to endure battle stress but also pressing financial questions about the affordability of war at all for Western governments.

5. Chris Dowrick vis

6. The research was carried out by Professor Carl Heneghan of Oxford University's Department of Primary Care Health Sciences and colleagues at the

independent Cochrane Collaboration, reported in the Oxford Science Blog on April 10 2014.

7. Professors Stanley Feldman and Vincent Marks: *Global warming and Other Bollocks (2009)*

THE JUSTICE FRANCHISE

1. R T Paget: *Manstein: His Campaigns and His Trial (1951)*

THE VICTIM FRANCHISE

2. For a brilliant expose of the legal dangers and social absurdities of this "cult of victimhood", read Barbara Hewson's article in *The Barrister* of February 25 2014.

3. Harold Bloom: The Western Canon (1994)

4. BBC Interview: April 11 2014

5. Judge David Tyzack, Western Morning News, July 1 2014

THE ENVIRONMENT FRANCHISE

1. UK Met Office statement of October 15 2012 in response to claims that Global Warming had stagnated for 16 years.

2. Decadal temperature change had averaged about 0.03% between 1997 and 2012, something which even the UK Met Office had to concede was negligible, although it warned that each decade since 1980 had been hotter than the previous one. True, but it did little to help the credibility of the UN's Intergovernmental Panel on Climate Change, the main cheer leader for environmental alarmism, whose composite models had predicted decadal increases of 0.2%. In fact, real global temperatures had increased by only a quarter of the amount predicted by the IPCC in 2007. Such poor forecasting would have ensured most CEO's dismissal. It only earned the IPCC more credibility by Western Governments, and more grant money.

3. The UK Met Office's document, *The Recent Pause in Global Warming (2) What are the Causes: July 2013)* suggests that the heat has been trapped under the sea. It was only one of 52 theories circulating in scientific circles about why Global warming had "paused".

4. The embarrassment of riches in terms of theories about why the climate scientists had got their predictions wrong, helped prompt a change in emphasis from Global Warming to Climate Change. In reality, they refer to two different things: one is rising global temperatures and the other is the climatic effect of those changes. But given the difficulty of rousing public panic about a planet that was inconsiderately hardly warming at all, it was easier to refer to Climate Change --- it made for better television images too.

5. UN's Intergovernmental Panel on Climate Change Fifth Assessment Report (AR5) 2013

6. Dr Gabriel Calzada Alvarez of Madrid's Juan Carlos University reported in 2009 that his research suggested that for every one job created in the Green sector, 2.2 jobs were destroyed elsewhere because of the rising cost of energy. The Business for Britain group, meanwhile, warned in 2014 that EU green policies were putting 1.5 million British jobs at risk through high energy costs.

7. The literature on this subject is vast. Suffice it here to merely drawn attention to some of the seminal work done in exploding the myth that this most egregious example of the scam, renewable energy, can make an

economically sustainable contribution to either carbon reductions or fossil fuel replacement.

David J C MacKay in his *Sustainable Energy Without the
Hot Air (2009)*, points out the impossibility of solar and
wind systems to make a substantive contribution to energy self-sufficiency in, for example, the UK. Dieter Helm
in *The Carbon Crunch (2012)* argues that the standby capacity of conventional generating fleets to accommodate
intermittent energy supply from renewables amounts to
a considerable subsidy to renewable technologies.

The exact scale of that cost had to await research
by Charles Frank of the Brookings Institution, published as the *Global Economy and Development Working
Paper 73 (2014)*. He carried out the first comprehensive
cost-benefit analysis of different energy technologies,
including the hidden subsidy. Frank determined that it
cost $188 432 to displace one MW per year of coal-
based electricity through solar technology and $25 333
through wind. Hydro power, conversely, gave a positive
value of $180 432, nuclear $318 569 and Gas Combined
$535 382.

The renewable energy lobbies furiously challenged
the numbers but had an uphill battle when confronted
by the empirical outcome of its policies as represented
by Germany where 50% of its electricity was generated by renewables by 2014.

8. The UK's Annual Fuel Poverty Statistics report 2014 stated that 10.4% of British households, 2.28 million of them, lived in fuel poverty as defined either by households paying above the national norm or because the cost of fuel they needed drove them below national poverty levels. Even given that developed world poverty levels are computer modelled notions, the report does indicate significant pain being taken by households to pay for energy, largely thanks to the additional costs and levies for renewable energy.

9. The UK Parliament's International Development Committee's report of June 2013 lays the blame for higher and more volatile world food prices squarely on the effects of biofuel demand. Ironically, the role of biofuels has led to one of the few rows between two franchises of supercrisis.org. The environmentalists punt biofuels. The poverty franchise points to its effects on food prices for poor people.

10. The price of UK coniferous hard wood rose by 50% in the decade to 2013, largely due to the demand for wood chippings for the heavily subsidised biomass industries. Similar reports came from the US where higher wood prices drove up the cost of low-income housing provision.

And Yet More Franchises

1. The extraordinary feature of numerous studies of social mobility is the arrogant and middle-class assumption that success can be measured only by academic qualification or financial success. Thus all the focus of numerous state interventions has been to take poor children and get them all to university. The projects inevitably fail. The major challenge in the developed world right now is to de-gear the elite's ludicrous expectations of children with limitations imposed by genetic heritability and to establish real benchmarks for success such as a tradable skill of any kind, stability of relationships, self sufficiency, community service etc. Small hope. This is not supercrisis.org's remit.

2. In May 2008 Myanmar was struck by Cyclone Nargis. The initial death toll was estimated to be 38 500 dead with 27 838 missing --- tragic but relatively small scale compared to later catastrophes and well within the country's capacity to manage. The isolationist military junta refused to allow Western aid agencies to enter the country. The response from supercrisis. org and the UN was of such an order that no serious person could be under any illusion but that this had

nothing to do with aiding victims and everything to do with protecting jobs in supercrisis.org.

3. A quick scan of the UN websites dealing with peacekeeping missions in 2013 reveal the not unsurprising fact that the biggest contributor of peacekeepers --- Pakistan at 8 283, Rwanda at 5 632 and Nepal at 5 208 --- are poor countries. In short, just another wealth transfer mechanism. At a broader level, not a single example of "peace keeping" since 1945 has had lasting success other than in countries where all warring parties were already committed to peace and in many cases were actively looking for an interlocutor. Where parties did not want peace, the interventions merely prolonged the agony, sometimes for years in what is now called frozen wars. Had the same interventionist impulse that exists today, and some mythical external force like the UN, existed in 1940, it is tempting to believe Europe would still be occupied by German forces, albeit restricted to secure areas monitored by a self-serving and entrenched international peace-keeping force.

4. The statistics come from the Global Slavery Index's Report of October 2013. The report is the product of the Walk Free Foundation which is linked to the Global Freedom Network which is linked to the ...... it just goes on and on.

MOPPING UP THE REST

1. The growth of the educational sector in a country like the UK is instructive. In 2000, professional teachers made up 71% of total school workforce. By 2010, after a decade of socialist government, they made up only 53%. The rest were made up of support teachers and administrators who in numerical terms had increased by 50% during the life of the socialist government. As already observed, the former had no authority to teach and the latter were unionists, so it was not surprising that British public education took such a plunge in the national league tables during this period. If one considers that 47% of Labour Party members in 2014 were "educationists", one can rapidly understand why British education had been sacrificed on the altar of the egalitarian ambitions of the socialists.

2. Judith Hackitt, the person in charge of the Health and safety Executive, warned that overzealous application of health and safety rules in schools, for example, were destroying c hildren's traditional playing ground activities and turning science lessons dull. (Reported in The Guardian, July 2 2011)

3. The row over immigrant entitlements in their countries of refuge became a touchstone of popular native

resistance in Western countries. The elites, in true Egalitarian Fantasy style, insisted objections to immigration were xenophobic, thus refusing to address the core issues of public service resources and threatened community identity. Their arrogance came back to bite them majestically with the explosive growth of major centre-right political parties organized around the issue of unrestrained immigration.

4. In 1960, for every one American on disability there were 134 workers. By 2012 there were 18. The number of people on disability allowance in the UK increased ten-fold from 1969 to 2013, according to the UK Office for National Statistics. Numbers provided by the UK's Coalition Government in 2012 indicated that only one in eight people claiming medical disability could be considered genuinely unable to do any work at all.

IN THE CRAZY ZONE

1. Composites of US Central Intelligence Agency and World Bank national accounts.

2. European Central Bank Working Paper (No 1233 August 2010).

3. The Community Reinvestment Act of 1977 and its various amendments forced US financial institutions to lend money to high risk communities, specifically the Afro-American and Hispanic communities.

4. Total Chinese Gross Capital Formation (formerly Fixed Domestic Investment) in the US jumped from USD 1.9Bn in 2007 to US17.1bn in 2012. By 2014, China was investing more in the US that the US in China. (World Bank national accounts data and OECD national accounts data)

5. Collateral Debt Obligations: "structural financial products that pool together cash flow-generating assets and repackages them into discrete tranches" (Investopedia). These products rose from £30 bn in 2003 to £225 bn in 2006. The collapse of this market led to huge losses in financial institutions around the world.

6. Pew Research: Global Attitudes: Project 46. April 15 2008

7. YouGov: July 2012. Other research by the University of Columbia: 2010, into the concepts of fairness and the extent to which they were culturally embedded came to the not unsurprising conclusion that the concept of fairness and the

principle of punishment for unfairness were much more embedded in higher income societies than lower ones. The point simply underscores the danger of assuming an equality of assumptions, particularly in regard to debt, by people from very unequal societies.

THE FINANCIAL COST IN A SNAPSHOT

1. The Economist World Debt Clock put world debt at $54 597 360 291 202 as of 1400 hours CET on November 1 2014 --- and growing.

2. The research by Daniel Shelter of the Boston Consulting Group, published in 2013, also showed that by 2012, 31 cents of every US Federal Government dollar spent was borrowed. Forty five per cent of this spend went towards Social Security and Health Care. In 2002 it was 25%.

3. The 2011 UK census showed that one sixth of the population were over 65 years of age.

4. If one includes pension accumulations, it was approximately $225 000, according to separate research by Friends Life and Scottish Widows.

5. By 2013 there were 14 million US citizens on disability allowances. The relaxation of medical eligibility requirements had contributed to a 45% growth in the number of male recipients and 36% for women in a decade. (US Social Security Services Administration: 2013)

6. The number of people in the UK on medical disability allowances increased from 325 600 in 1969 to 1 783 900 in 1995 under a Conservative government and thence to 3.3 million in 2013 thanks to the socialists, according to official statistics.

7. Social welfare spend in the EU was accounting for over half of the world's total public welfare spend by 2013. The US claimed 31% and China four per cent (*Social Protection Budgets in the Crisis in the EU, European Commission Working Paper 1/2013 by Olivier Bontout and Terezie Lokajklova*)

8. The rate of annual increase in real per capita GDP has been in decline for more than four decades. The median rate had fallen from four per cent per year in the 1960's to just 0.02% after 2008. It has recovered marginally in the UK and USA but the EU remains on a downward path. (US Central Intelligence Agency World Book) The most terrifying numbers relate to the growing proportion of households in the developed world who take out more in benefits than they

pay back in taxes. This very significant shift has had major policy implications and has brought the welfare system across the developed world to the brink of bankruptcy.

9. The Centre for Policy Studies in the UK, using Office for National Statistics, estimated that 53.4% of households in the UK took out more in benefits than they returned in taxes. The bottom three income quintiles were all in negative territory.

10. The same survey revealed that only one of the seven regions in the UK contributed more in taxes than it took out in taxes. That was the south-east with London at its heart.

11. University College, London published in The Economic Journal November 2014

12. The US Tax Policy Center put the number of Americans not paying Federal tax at 46.4% in 2011. Presidential hopeful Mitt Romney referred to it in a leaked video which was subsequently published by Mother Jones in September 2012. In the video he referred to this class as entitlement driven people who made no contribution to the country. He was pilloried but was substantially right. UK Office for National Statistics: October 2014.

13. UK Office of National Statistics

14. Research by *Vouchercloud* and reported in *HR Grapevine* in its November 2013 edition.

15. In 2013, 131 million working days were lost in the UK to illness with the worst offenders in the public service. In the same year the US economy lost $84 b due to illness, according to a Gallup and Healthways Survey of May 2013.

16. The investigations were controversial. Some research suggested children were spending more time than their parents.

17. For a chilling insight into the effect of social media sites, it is worth reading Nicholas Carr's *The Shallows: What the Internet is Doing To Our Brains* (Norton:2010). His thesis is that the internet has overwhelmed the literate mind by destroying our capacity to store sufficient data for deep thoughts in favour of a fragmented collection of information and ideas. The internet has literally rewired our brains. David Boddy, chairman of the Society of Heads representing 100 private schools in the UK, has meanwhile warned that a generation of internet- obsessed children are losing their powers of concentration. (The Daily Telegraph:

March 4 2013). Baroness Greenfield, Professor of Pharmocology at Oxford University and a leading neuroscientist, warned that social media were creating children with an obsession about feed-back, poor self-control, short attention-span and little empathy. (The Daily Telegraph, October 17, 2012).

THE END OF INNOVATION?

1. Refer to Clark: *The Son Also Rises* (2013). The remarkable thing emerging from this research was the capacity of those with the innate ability and their succeeding generations to hold onto their status and wealth through generations. Similarly, those without the capacity were remarkable by the slowness with which they were able to rise.

2. It is worth reading Governor Alan Greenspan's address to the Economic Club of New York on January 13 2000 to see his concern about the net wealth effect.

3. Erik Brynjolfsson and Andrew McAfee: *The Second Machine Age* (2014)

THE PRODUCTIVITY CONUNDRUM

1. Total Factor Productivity (FTP): "A measure of the efficiency of all inputs to a production process. Increases in FTP result usually from technological innovations or improvements". (BusinessDictionary.com). Some estimates suggest FTP contributes up to 60% of economic growth which is why its diminution has such dire impacts.

2. A report by the Institute for Economic Research at the University of Munich in 2007 perceptively argued that the slow down to TFP could at least be partly attributed to a slowing quality of labour, rather than simply capital. *Changes in Human Capital: Implications for Productivity Growth in the Euro Area* by Guido Schwerdt and Jarkko Turunen, Working Paper No 53, 2007.

3. The investor and UK columnist Roger Bootle has used this phrase a number of times to flag his concern about the lack of productivity in developed world countries.

4. Research by Robert Gordon of North western University shows that annual productivity increases in the US in the 1950's was 2.5%. In the 1970's it dropped to two per cent. In the 2000's it tumbled to one per cent. In the

immediate aftermath of the financial crisis of 2008, it fell to 0.4% before slightly recovering. (*The Economist: Briefing: January 12 2013*)

THE EGALITARIAN FANTASY FEEDS INEQUALITY

1. The common measure of inequality within a society is the Gini Coefficient where a score of 0 means everybody is equal and a score of 1 means one person owns everything. The OECD coefficient grew from 0.29 to 0.32 in the 25 years prior to 2013. The US's coefficient rose from 0.34 in 1985 to 0.38 in 2008. In the UK it went from 0.32 to 0.34. Even the Scandinavian countries, icons of equality, saw growing inequality. All of this, of course, occurred during a time of unprecedented social investment. One would have thought that even the Left would have begun to question the efficacy of its redistributive model. It did not --- it predictably went after the wealth creators.

2. The UK Office for National Statistics reported in March 2014 that although life expectancy levels had generally narrowed, there were still stark differences between various parts of the country, some of them growing.

3. A controversial book by Professor Tyler Cowen en-
    titled *Average is Over: Powering America Beyond The Age of
    the Great Stagnation: 2013,* paints a picture in which an
    elite 10 to 15% of Americans will have the brains and
    self-discipline to master new technologies and create
    enormous wealth. The rest will bump along providing
    services to the super rich or falling between the cracks
    on stagnant or even falling wages.

    Charles Murray, in his book Coming Apart: The
    State of White America 1960 to 2010, argues that
    there is a small group of super bright and rich peo-
    ple in the US, about five per cent, who live isolated,
    stable and fulfilling lives, as will their children and
    grandchildren. At the other end of the scale lies a layer
    comprising 20% of white Americans who are disinte-
    grating through sloth, promiscuity, loss of values and
    disappearance of community. His concern is that this
    group will simply be converted to a welfare project, as
    happened in the UK.

4. Oxford University Study published in *British Journal of
    Sociology* reported Telegraph November 12-18

5. Thomas Piketty: *Capital in the 21st Century (2013).*
    The foremost articulators of this Egalitarian
    Fantasy were Richard Wilkinson and Kate Pickett
    in *The Spirit Level*, a must-read for the redistributive

political classes. Their argument is that countries with high degrees of inequality are less successful than ones with lower levels of inequality due largely to epigenetic effects originally caused by inequality. The answer is to tax the rich more and pump the money in the direction of the poor. The methodology of their work was exploded by Christopher Snowden in his *The Spirit Level Delusion* (2010) in which he exposed serious errors of methodology. More to the point, it is an a priori argument. Countries which are successful are more equal to begin with, genetically and homogeneously, while those that are unsuccessful are more unequal to begin with.

6. Report by the Institute of Education's Research Centre on Life and Learning: 2014.

7. Inland Revenue Service numbers showed that by 2013, the top one per cent of US taxpayers was contributing 36.9% of Federal tax, the top five per cent 57.1% and the top 10% 68%. The bottom 50% was paying 3.3%. Although the numbers roughly approximated wealth distribution, the hard fact was that an ever higher proportion of taxes were being picked up at the top and a smaller amount being recovered from the middle and bottom. Median USA taxpayers saw their contribution

to the total drop from 19.4% in 1979 to 11.2% in 2010. The US tax Foundation declared US tax to be the most progressive in the world and a report by the US Congressional Budget Office Report of 2014 showed that the top 40% of tax payers in the US were paying *all* the taxes.

8. Institute for Fiscal Studies: Public Finance Bulletin: January 2015

9. Average Life Expectancy in East Dorset in 2011 for a male was 82.9 years, according to the Office For National Statistics. In Glasgow it was 72.6 years. Is it mischievous to point to the fact that East Dorset has been historically held by Conservatives and Glasgow by socialists?

10. 149   Gordon Brown, the UK's least popular socialist Prime Minister, frequently boasted about how he had "lifted" nearly a million children out of poverty. He had done no such thing. By giving extended tax credit he had created a notional value to the intervention which had little impact on the lifestyles, prospects or character of the poor. Where there was a cash enhancement, it was immediately monetised.

11. The BBC 2013 Great British Class Survey comprising 161 000 participants said the old class differentiations

of upper, middle and working class no longer worked. They identified seven groups: elites, established middle class, technical middle class, newly affluent workers, traditional working class, emergent service workers and the precariat or precarious proletariat. The important point was that this new definition finally established the real fault lines in modern society: the high wealth and high skilled components, or those on the way to joining them, and the low wealth and low skilled groups. The gap between the two has grown enormously. US Census numbers would indicate that the equivalent proportion of "precariats" is about 16% of the population.

12. An online education business, Learn Direct, claimed that school leavers in British schools in 2013 were worse equipped for the workplace than those who left in 1851. The report focussed on basic skills like needlework, cooking, joinery and tinkering which provided entry points for Victorian children to the job market.

13. The epidemic of obesity in particular in the UK, is worthy of a study in itself; a classic example of what happens when genetics meets inappropriate social policies. Adipose tissue is intended to create a reserve of fat for energy during adverse climatic seasons. This excess was rapidly burnt off through the unrelenting

drudge of our forebears ' lives, thus keeping relative weight equilibrium. Absence the drudge, add welfare payments, access to low value food and lack of capacity to understand the importance of nutrition and, voilà, obesity on a horrific scale, particularly amongst lower income groups. The next move, in perfect accord with Egalitarian Fantasy principles, was to elevate obesity to the norm: major clothing chains proudly presented overweight mannequins to make women feel more "comfortable" in their excess. Support groups for the obese flourished. Slim people, those who watched their diet and exercised, again following the rules, became regarded as the despised exceptions.

14. Gregory Clark: *The Son Also Arises:* 2014

15. Tyler Cowen: *Average is Over:2013*

16. Research by Dr Michael Woodley and published in the journal *Intelligence* in 2014 claims that reaction times, a marker for general intelligence (G2, not to be confused with IQ), had declined from Victorian times from about 182 milliseconds to 250 milliseconds in men and from 187 milliseconds to 277 in women. This translates to a decrease in general intelligence equivalent to 1.23 IQ points a decade since 1880. The reason, suggests Dr Woodley, is a reverse in the process of natural selection as the most intelligent people

have fewer children while there are higher survival rates amongst people with the least favourable genes.

17. The OECD Report on a survey of 166 000 participants in October 2013 confirmed the catastrophic decline in public education in many developed world countries.

18. The research was carried out by Grant Tomkinson of the University of South Australia and the American Heart Foundation and reported in 2013. It found children in the nine to 17 age group would on average take 90 seconds longer to run a mile than would children from 30 years ago. Heart related fitness has declined five per cent each decade since 1975. Today's children are on average 15% less fit than their parents.

19. Research by the University College in London and published in Archives of Disease in Childhood: 2013.

20. Daily Telegraph July 11 2014

21. Research published by *UK Active:* 2013

22. Some intriguing research by Professor Anna Goodman of the London School of Hygiene and Tropical Medicine published in *Proceedings of the Royal Society:* 2012 suggested that although middle-class

families might have brighter children, they had fewer
of them. It was thus the lower status groups who were
evolutionary winners because they were growing in
numbers. Darwin's theory of the survival of the fit-
test had become survival of the fattest, thanks to the
Egalitarian Fantasy.

23. Official figures indicated 120 000 households had been
identified as having severe problems. More alarmist
reports claimed they were costing the taxpayer £30
bn a generation in social service support.

24. Numbers released by the Ministry of Justice in the
UK in 2012 showed that 100 000 criminals had more
than 15 convictions. The number of repeat offenders
as a proportion of the total had increased from 18% in
2001 to 31.2% in 2012 while the number of first time
offenders had plummeted.

25. The research was carried out by Amir Sariaslan
of the Karolinska Institute in Stockholm and published in the *British Journal of Psychiatry*, involved
tracking back on the records of half a million subjects born between 1989 and 1993. The research
showed that mere social migration did not mitigate the predisposition to criminality. Research by
Exeter and Birmingham Universities for the Office
of the Children's Commissioner in 2012, meanwhile,

showed large numbers of juvenile offenders had neural developmental issues such as brain damage or severe impairment of their reading, speech, language and learning abilities.

26. Professor Adrian Raine, Professor of Criminology at the University of Pennsylvania, writes in his book *The Anatomy of Violence,* that both minor and serious criminals exhibit different patterns of brain activity from normal people.

THE FEMINIST FRANCHISE

1. Professor James Flynn Rising IQ in the 21st Century (2012)

2. Research by Queen's College in New York and augmented by further work by James Chung of Reach Advisors using US Census numbers, found in a 2014 report that unmarried, childless women under 30 years of age earned an average eight per cent more than their male peers in 147 out of the 150 major US cities surveyed. Such work definitively crushes the feminist argument that women are discriminated against *as women.* They earn less and are disadvantaged in terms of promotions because

on average they are less productive and work less. The causes, many of them utterly legitimate, are a different issue and not relevant to the *economic* impact of driving through affirmative action gender quotas.

3. The UK's General Lifestyle Survey of 2013 found a stabilisation of marriages amongst white collar and professionals. Blue collar workers were going the other way. In 2001, 53% of workers were married. It is now 44%.

4. The Office for National Statistics reported in 2013 that men lost 1.6% of their working hours to illness. Women lost 2.6% --- 62% more downtime.

5. A study by the UK Department of Education in 2014 revealed the even more sobering fact that in families which could live on one salary (i.e. the male's), women were leaving employment altogether. Sixty per cent of middle class women would give up full-time work if they could afford it and 40% would give up work altogether. The results were a convincing rebuttal of the proposition by the Egalitarian Fantasy that equality of work opportunity overrode biological imperatives.

6. It is perhaps illustrative that although there are reams of research about women's attitude to work, there is a paucity of such investigations regarding men. Either this is because it is considered an unimportant issue or, more likely, it is simply assumed from a weight of other indices that men in employment overwhelmingly want to work.

7. An article in the Harvard Business Review, Why Men Still Get More Promotions Than Men, by Ibarra, Carter and Silva in September 2010 refers to 83% of women having received mentorship and only 76% for men.

8. A 2015 report by the UK Department of Health is worth quoting in full: "(The) gender balance in general practice has shifted due to a significant increase in the number of women becoming GP's. This so-called feminisation of the workforce necessitates an increase in the number of trainees in order to maintain the current full-time equivalent workforce as women are more likely to work part-time." One of the suggestions was to increase incentives for people to become doctors. Problem was that 16 000 out of 40 000 British doctors already earned more than £100 000 a year, already an insupportable cost for

the NHS. Here, then, was a perfect example of the hidden cost of affirmative employment: a cost never considered or calculated. (Reported in The Daily Telegraph: February 26 2015)

9. An intriguing European Union Commission Report entitled *Parents At Work: Men and Women Participating In The Labour Force of April 2014* determined that 70% of women of economically active age were in work compared to 85% of men. The research also established the fact that across the board women's willingness to work declined with the number of children they reared. This is so utterly predictable that it hardly needs research. What is astonishing is that this biological and laudable imperative is regarded by the Egalitarian Fantasists as aberrational and to be dealt with by establishing yet more quotas for women in work.

10. A study by University College of London in 2013 found that half of the foreign doctors working in the UK failed to meet the professional requirements imposed on indigenous doctors. The story can be repeated across the developed world.

11. The discovery by Project 28-40, supported by Opportunity Now (2014) predictably blames lack of management imagination in deploying flexitime as

the culprit for the tensions between flexitime workers and non-parent workers. The reality is more mundane: non-parent women object to having to pick up the slack for women who believe they can balance their parental against their work investment without cost to either, or their colleagues.

12. Research by the Resolution Foundation found that between 1968 and 2008 women accounted for three times more of working families' income growth than men. (The Economist March 16 2013)

13. Independent Resolution Foundation: *Low Pay Britain (2013)* Research by Strategy &, formerly Booz & Company, in 2013 indicated that one third of women appointed to be CEO's in top companies were forced out because of performance. Only a quarter of males were. The research also established the close link about the number of men promoted internally and thus better positioned for success as opposed to the number of women imported from outside.

14. Harvard Business Review: *Why Men Still Get More Promotions Than Women,* By H Ibarra, N Carter and C Silva, September 2010) together with Levo League Research report of May 2 2013.

15. The UK's Office for National Statistics showed that by 2011, 66% of divorces were initiated by women, slightly down on the previous number of 70%.

16. The same source provided evidence to show that the "unreasonableness" of the women partner as a ground for divorce had risen six-fold in forty years. The feminists insisted that this was because women were becoming more "assertive". Assertiveness of women is not a ground for divorce: unreasonableness is. And in parenthesis, over-assertiveness of men is now a criminal offence in the UK.

17. Department for Business Innovation and Skills: Daily Telegraph January 27 2014

18. Patricia Morgan: Farewell to The Family: (London Institute of Economic Affairs 1999)

19. US National Center for Health Statistics Data Brief No 18 (May 2009)

20. The list of social pathologies in young people resulting from the breakdown of family life is endless. Herewith a few: children in broken homes are three times more likely to run away (Report for the Children's Society in 2011); children from broken homes are nine times more likely to commit crimes

(UK Works and Pensions Minister in a speech on November 4 2010); step fathers are likely to abuse their step children at a rate materially above that of biological fathers (USA's National Center for Health Research 2010).

21. Health care organisations for the elderly reported a fall of one third in health care visits to elderly people in their homes between 2010 and 2013 in the UK. The egalitarian promise of health care in every elderly person's home could just not match the rising demands and costs of the service.

22. Research by Scottish Widows in 2011 indicated that in the UK 43% of people above the age of 60 were living alone although 2011 Census statistics suggested it was about 31%. The issue is admirably covered in The Economist (November 15 2014) entitled A Nordic Mystery. It was no mystery of course. The biological imperative could not be negated, not even by Scandinavian egalitarian fantasy.

23. The issue is particularly alive in Sweden where the Government is piloting a "cash for care" project in which money is paid directly to mothers to ostensibly pay for daily child care. Opponents, including many from the Left, claim it incentivises women to step out of work early.

24. See (2) above

25. Advertising Age White Paper: The Rise of The Real Mom by Narissa Miley and Ann Mack, July 2009 reported that while 57% of males rated a career "very important", only 36% of women did. Again, 69% of women rated parenthood "very important" versus 42% of males.

IMMIGRATION AND THE EGALITARIAN FANTASY

1. Robert Putnam in his book *Bowling Alone: 2001* accumulated significant data showing that diverse communities had lower levels of personal trust, community, civic mindedness, voluntarism and confidence than homogenous ones. The evidence was simply brushed off by the political classes --- remember former Prime Minister Gordon Brown's infamous "bigoted woman" comment during the 2010 UK General Elections.

2. Social Integration Commission UK, Report 2014

3. The UK Electoral Commission's Final Report and Recommendations on Electoral Fraud (June 2014)

acknowledges that 16 electoral districts are vulnerable to fraud. All of them have high densities of immigrant populations. The report also acknowledges high incidences of fraud amongst communities of the Indian subcontinent, primary Pakistani and Bangladeshi. The report typically declines to quantify its scale.

4. Surveys of the surnames of those convicted of electoral fraud in the UK show they are overwhelmingly of the Indian subcontinent.

5. Official statistics indicate that 55% of marriages in the UK by Pakistani-descended individuals are by consanguinity, mainly between first cousins. The potentially damaging physical and mental consequences of this are widely published. In the case of the UK, the rate of physical abnormality of the offspring from such Pakistani-descended unions is double the UK average. The genetic danger inherent in this custom of marriage by consanguinity is widely and publicly acknowledged, including senior members of the Pakistani community.

6. Some research indicates that more than 70% of Pakistanis in the UK are related by blood. (Department of Obstetrics and Gynaecology, Faculty of Clinical Sciences,, University College of London: 2013)

7. The UK Parliament's Report On Underachievement By White Working Class Children (June 2014) reports that 32% of poor white children achieve five good GCSE grades compared to 42% of black Caribbean children and 61% of disadvantaged Indian ones. Given that the grades are in any case grossly inflated, one begins to understand how badly equipped poor white children in the UK are to make their way in life. Professor Simon Burgess of Bristol University suggested in his research, published in 2014, that schools with large numbers of migrants did better than mostly white British children because the migrants had a better work ethic. Obviously: they had not been corrupted by the Egalitarian Fantasy.

8. The reasons adduced by the Egalitarian franchises for this failure are numerous and almost wholly erroneous. The reason white working class children do so badly is because the Egalitarian Fantasy, exemplified by the Welfare State, socialist nihilism and dumbed-down education, has eviscerated their family and community life. They are ripe for association with the lowest levels of the immigrant classes and for adoption of their marginalized life-styles.

9. Paul Collier's book *Exodus* (2013) resolutely steers clear of any discussion of genetics but is still a masterful exposure of the key liberal fantasies about the merits of both unrestricted immigration and multiculturalism. His argument is that nobody benefits from rapid and uncontrolled immigration: neither host countries, countries of origins, migrants or indigenes. In short, naïve egalitarianism only creates new problems. The right-wing would argue it was not a new problem and would no doubt ask us to reflect on these words in the Anglo Saxon Chronicles in 959 about Abbot Aetherwold: *One grave fault, however, was all too characteristic of him/ Namely he was fond of foreign, vicious customs/ And introduced heathen practices too eagerly, Into this land: he invited foreigners hither/ And encouraged harmful elements to enter the country.*

10. *The Economic Journal* November 2014 University College London

11. *Migration Watch* tracked UK opinions regarding immigration back to 1964 and showed that a constant theme has been the opposition by a majority of British people to further migration.

12. Migration Watch June 2014.

AND THE CULTURE

1. Harold Bloom: The Western Canon (1994)

POLITICAL EFFECTS

1. Figures from the 2013 American Time Use Survey showed those with bachelor's degrees worked two hours a day longer than those with high school diplomas --- eight hours a week, equal to another full working day a week. The number of degreed US men working more than 50 hours a week rose from 24% in 1979 to 28% in 2006 but fell for drop-outs. There are two drivers here: the earnings for high level work were attractive enough to make people want to work more at the top end and the pervasive availability of welfare support was driving down working hours at the bottom end. It was a classic illustration of how the Egalitarian Fantasy is increasing inequality. The research was backed up by an Oxford University study published in its *Sociology Working Papers (2014)*

2. Francis Fukuyama:, *The End of History and the Last Man (1992)* and Samuel Huntington *Clash of Civilizations and the Remaking of the World Order (1992)*

3. The topic is worthy of a book in itself, and indeed has been for many, many books. Suffice here simply to observe that the Euro Zone was founded on the egalitarian belief that a single currency could serve the interests of a number of countries vastly divided by levels of wealth, culture, work ethic and resources. Once the single currency came under threat as it did in 2008, there was simply no way to manage its damaging fallouts than by internal devaluation --- a reduction in state expenditure which has sparked internal resistance.

4. How "squeezed" this class really is, or ever was, is in fact a matter of speculation. The UK Office of National Statistics Household Expenditure Survey for 2013 showed that spend on fun things --- entertainment, recreation, alcohol, tobacco, drugs, hotels --- as a proportion of total household expense had actually increased during the recession. Whatever the "squeezed" middle class were cutting back on, it was not *la dolce vita*.

5. Parties outside the historic mainstream ones in Europe drew roughly a quarter of votes in the 2014 European Parliament elections: UKIP 27.5% in Britain; Front National 24.8% in France; Five Star Movement; 25% in Italy, Syriza 25.6% in Greece. Those hoping these levels of support were aberrational were in for a disappointment: subsequently the Party of the Alternative in Germany doubled its European elections support

in regional elections in Thuringia and UKIP gained two Parliamentary seats in a two adjacent by-elections with a humiliating defeat for both the conservative and socialist candidates.

6. Avi Tuschman: *Our Political Nature*: 2013

7. Tony Blair holds the dubious distinction of having passed 54% more laws during his tenure than Margaret Thatcher, a total of 26 849 laws, according to the online legal information service, Sweet & Maxwell. The vast majority sought to extend the purview of the state into the private lives of the citizens. Many of these laws were in response to public pressure on specific, ad hoc issues. It was law making on the run --- and its consequences for personal freedom were devastating.

8. Party Political Broadcast: June 4 1945

9. The order was granted by the Court of Protection after an application by the Essex social services in November 2013. It was unprecedented and raised questions in the UK Parliament.

10. The growth of intrusive surveillance and extraordinary powers to maintain stability in the developed world is a direct consequence of the original weakening

of effective policing by the Egalitarian Fantasy and its host of human rights franchises. Those franchises, having created the circumstances, now reap the benefit --- more fantasy jobs to protect the victims of the "oppressive" regimes created by the fantasy in the first place.

11. Gilles de Leuzes: *Short Essay: Postscript On The Societies of Control (1990)*

THE BROADER IMPLICATIONS

1. This process of consolidating trade flows outside the traditional north-south patterns underwent a dramatic acceleration in 2014 as Russia and China sought to strengthen ties. A slew of trade agreements, most focusing on oil and gas trades, were concluded, even as Western sanctions against Russia intensified. The message was obvious: two very powerful world players were creating a new game to which the West was not invited.

2. In October 2014, the European Central Bank was finally forced to commit a trillion Euros to buying back government bonds in an effort to revive European economies and forestall deflation. The move opened

Germany to huge risk as it was the major underwriter of bonds on behalf of all Europe.

3. Ironically, Russian adventurism has given NATO a new lease of life, away from intervention in obscure foreign wars and back towards its original mission: protecting Western Europe from Russia. Now, of course, the job has just got bigger: it is the whole of Eastern Europe it also has to protect thanks to the enlargement of the EU. But while the Brussels bureaucrats were delighted to welcome its new members for ideological reasons, they failed to take the elementary precaution of ensuring that it had the capacity to defend them in a tough neighbourhood. The Americans have their doubts: in numerous leaked communications they have railed against the refusal of European states to shoulder their responsibilities in building a military capacity to oppose continental aggression.

4. A classic example of this myopic Western middle-class view of the way that other folk should behave, but rarely do, is found in the role of the International Court of Justice. It was premised on the solid middle-class view that tyrants in developing world countries would behave better if they feared retribution. It had the opposite effect. The lesson that tyrants drew, particularly in Africa and the Middle East, was that if they came to the end of their constitutional terms

they should extend them and if they lost elections they should subvert them and if there was a rebellion they should brutally crush it. The number of states recorded as "unfree" by human rights bodies soared. Thus ended a promising period of peaceful democratic transfers in Africa based on bipartisan if hardly transparent "deals" between incoming and outgoing leaders. With the advent of the International Court of Justice this became irrelevant: a newly elected leader had a better than even chance of shunting an opponent off to the Court in a tumbril. What need for a smoky room deal about the divvying up of national resources for personal enrichment? Incumbent leaders, unsurprisingly, realised this --- and resisted leaving office.

5. In Smith and Others (Appellant) v Ministry of Defence (Defendant) before the UK High Court, the Judges decided by a majority that a claim for damages by the families of people killed in foreign wars by UK soldiers could proceed. Lord Mancer and other Judges warned that the decision must inevitably lead to the "judicialisation" of war. In the end it would be impossible for sovereign states to defend their vital interests by war. Just the way the Egalitarian Fantasists wanted it.

6. Surely one of the great ironies of recent history has been the way that the European Union's determined

denigration of the integrity of the sovereign nation state has led to its logical outcome: the growth of secessionist tendencies throughout Europe, much of it fed by huge transfers of money from Brussels. Amongst the regions most affected: Scotland, Wales, Cornwall, (UK) Veneto, South Tyrol, Sardinia (Italy), Catalonia, Galicia, Aragon, The Basque Region (Spain), Corsica, Brittany, Occitania, Alsace, Savoy (France), Flanders (Belgium), Bavaria (Germany), Silesia (Poland), Frisia (Netherlands and Germany) and Aaland (Finland). A controversial Deutsche Bank report in early 2015 suggested that certain regions in Spain, Italy, Belgium, the UK and France would be economically better off if they took independence. It would be absurd to suggest all these regions are just waiting to spring loose from their historic connections with their metropolitan hosts but it is equally certain that the more European national states lose a sense of core identity, the more will such regional aspirations grow. The astonishing 45% of Scots who voted to separate from the UK in 2014 did so for one main reason: British leaders through decades had failed to offer them a sense of over-arching national identity and pride sufficient to counter-weight the pull of ancestry, big welfare budgets and tribal loyalties. Again, the Egalitarian Fantasy has taken us back, not forward.

THE PUSH BACK BEGINS

1. The financial crisis of 2008 merely accelerated a long-standing trend of stagnating middle and lower level wages. The UK suffered a 6.1% loss in real earnings between 2007 and 2012. The USA's wages remained stagnant until 2012 when they saw a slight uptick, according to International Monetary und statistics. Apart from France and Germany, all EU countries saw a stagnation of wages, the former protected by its economic strength and the latter perilously supported by interventionist policies.

2. The Skills and Employment Survey funded by the Economic and Social Research Council and the UK Commission for Employment and Skills (May 2013), showed British workers felt more insecure in their jobs than they had for 20 years. Tellingly, public sector workers for the first time felt more at risk than private sector ones. Predictably, the media and the supercrisis.org franchises focused on the victimology of it all. Less reported were the benefits to the whole society in terms of workers trying harder to hold onto jobs, reduced absenteeism, larger investments in personal growth and so on.

3. South African Sunday Times, September 21 2014

4. The 2008 crisis destroyed an estimated $34tr in world wide wealth. USA household wealth plummeted from $65.8tr in Q1 2007 to $49.40tr in Q1 2009. The biggest hit was in property prices which lost 30% of their value in this period. (Rooseveld Institute: The Crisis of Wealth Destruction: May 2011) This wealth was "bubble wealth" and its creation, I would argue, was directly attributable to the need to feed the Egalitarian Fantasy.

5. The US Office of Research Integrity investigated reported clinical tests between 1990 and 2003. They found in 40% of the reports the conclusions were totally wrong or significantly incorrect. Other research suggested that anything up to 80% of the research that found its way into the popular media was either withdrawn, disproved or never taken further.

6. An interesting hit on this is the Report, *Public Trust In The News*, by S Coleman, S Anthony and D Morrison (Reuters Institute for the Study of Journalism (2009) It records the very clear disconnect between the media's play of a story and the way ordinary people receive it. A large part of this, I believe, relates to the growing scepticism by the broad public about the may western media promotes the marketing output of supercrisis.org.

7. Office For National Statistics, reported in The Daily Telegraph, Friday May 30 2014 plus UK Census 2011.

8. The UK's General Lifestyle Survey reported in 2013 the encouraging news that the proportion of marriages that dissolved quickly had fallen to 1970 levels and the proportion of families headed by a single parent dropped from 27% in 2002 to 22% in 2011. But this was still not saying much. In 1945 there were 16 000. In 2012 117 000. The number of marriages had collapsed to the level of Victorian times.

9. Paul Tough, in his book *How Children Succeed: Grit, Curiosity and the Hidden Power of Character* (2013) argues that all the research indicates that key non-cognitive personality attributes like grit, determination, perseverance and discipline are at least as important as intelligence in making for successful humans. He does not call them Victorian values but of course they are: the bedrock on which successful Western nations were built before they were swept away by the Egalitarian Fantasy.

10. Britain's Conservative Coalition of 2010 to 2015 can no doubt take comfort from the fact that they have presided over the fastest growing economy in Europe during their term. Less impressive is its success in

reducing the debt overhang. Its failure was directly related to its refusal to abolish the welfare state, constrain the unions, reconfigure the bureaucracy and end foreign moral imperialism, an astonishing lapse given that the crisis left by the socialist government in 2010 had opened the door for radical reforms which would have enjoyed majority support. Instead, the Coalition got the worst of all worlds: debt, UKIP, entanglements in messy foreign wars and, bizarrely, a still strong socialist opposition.